Symphony

Conducting Supercharged Organizational Performance

Pierre Mourier

Cover design by Jim Walton. Cover illustration by Andrew George.

ISBN number: 978-0-578-13871-8
First Edition, 2014

Published by SG Press

Dedication

This book is dedicated to:

Jeanne Marie, Jean-Paul, and Collette

without whom absolutely none of this would be possible.

Thank you to Jimmy Walton, who is one of the most gifted graphic designers I have ever worked with, not only for the work on this book, but also for the work on the Stractics Group brand. Thank you to Christina Di Martino, the Editor on this project. Her spectacular use of the English language saved me again and again. Also thank you to Andrew George who designed the cover illustration.

Thank you to clients and colleagues who I have had the good fortune to work with over the years and who I have learnt from and who have had an impact (knowingly or unknowingly) on how this manuscript came together and how the Symphony methodology was developed. In particular I would like to thank Mike DeNoma, CEO of glh Hotels, who continues to support our innovation in driving human and organizational performance, and who I continuously learn from. And finally, to Geary Rummler, who was the inventor of process thinking as far as I am concerned, and whom I had the pleasure to work with directly and learn from.

Contents

Chapter 1
The Epiphany

He stared at the plaque on his office wall...

Just as the phone rang, shaking him from his thoughts "Your meeting with Eric has been rescheduled for tomorrow, Jim," Eric's secretary, Pamela Swickley said, allowing her voice to identify her.

"What time Pammy?"

She detected the despair in his voice. "Let me see, hmm, four o'clock. Will that work for you?"

"It's as good a time as any, I guess."

Spencer Services Company

Jim Robertson
Most Valuable Player

Superior Managerial
Performance Award
2010

Eric Struber, Jr.
President

She detected his air of resignation. "Things aren't good right now, are they Jim?"

Pamela had been working for Spencer Services Company since its humble beginnings—when Eric Struber, Sr. began operating a small engineering services company out of his garage, out of necessity more than desire. Recently laid off from one of the large engineering firms suffering the effects of the 1974 energy crisis, the start-up was a matter of survival.

Early on, Spencer Services secured a large government contract, and grew quickly from that point. Within five years, the company owned the eight-story building housing its offices. The staff had grown to over 100. By the time the "old man," as he was affectionately called, retired in 2012, the company had grown to a powerful organization with operations in 24 countries and several thousand employees. Following a brief transition period the founder's son, Eric, had taken over the chair in the corner office, and carried the title of president of Spencer Services.

Eric enjoyed a high regard of respect. Everyone who worked at the company admired his great people skills. Jim considered him a real "stand-up" guy. Despite everyone's affection for Eric, however, things had been on a downward slide for the past couple of years.

Jim Robertson had been with the company for eight years. He began as a supervisor in one of the manufacturing divisions, but company officials quickly recognized his talents, and even financed his MBA studies. Jim now headed up one of the smaller companies, called Spencer, Inc., as its general manager. Spencer produced and marketed a line of automation products for the engineering industry.

"Yeah, Pammy, things could be a lot better right now," Jim answered. "We just don't seem to be able to get a handle on the quality problems we're having. And sales seem to have fallen through the floor into this abyss. Its not like the competitors are doing much better, are they?" He sighed loudly. "You know what beats me the most, Pammy?"

"No. What?"

"I don't think I could possibly find better people than those who work for Spencer. There are always a few bad apples, of course, but overall..." he paused. "I'm worried about how much longer we can continue putting this pressure on them. There just never seem to be enough hours in the day. Anyway, Pammy, enough of my complaining. You're always so patient and willing to listen. Changing the meeting to tomorrow gives me some more time to come up with a plan," he knew he sounded more hopeful than he was.

Jim liked talking to Pamela. Besides being the CEO's personal assistant, she was known as the company's mother hen. She took Jim under her wing right from the beginning.

"Don't worry Jim," she consoled. "I know you'll come up with something for tomorrow—you always do. And remember, work isn't everything. Make sure you pay attention to that cute wife of yours, and those delicious kids. You can't keep working like this." The concern in her voice was audible.

"Thanks Pammy, you're sweet. I'll see you tomorrow."

Jim glanced again at the plaque as he hung up the phone. He fondly remembered the day Eric Struber, Sr. presented it to him—one of the last duties the old man had performed before retiring. Receiving the honor was a big deal in the Spencer organization, and it came with more than a plaque to hang on the wall. A three-week paid vacation in Bora Bora was a part of the award. Jim and Jill took the trip. It was a wonderful vacation. They snorkeled, slept late and lazily relaxed in the sun watching the wind blow its song through the palm fronds. Waking up in the morning to the sound of the waves lapping the shore, and great seafood dinners under the open sky seemed like a fantasy. He showed Jill Orion's belt and the Southern Cross in the night sky as they walked on the beach under the protective cover of the Milky Way.

The phone rang again. Jim, who realized that he had been just about to start a major round of daydreaming, instantly jumped back to the stark reality of the cloudy afternoon at work.

"Robertson," he answered with an annoyed ring in his voice.

"Hi honey, it's me," the voice seemed to ignore his cross tone. "Happy birthday, my love. I just wanted to remind you about our plans tonight. We'll meet at the restaurant at six sharp, right?"

Jill always seemed to sound upbeat, even in the middle of despair. Jim wondered how his wife managed her consistently positive attitude. Today was his 36th birthday, and in her true nature, she had planned what she thought would be a pleasant and de-stressing evening for him. Following an early dinner at his favorite restaurant, they would see the Tchaikovsky ballet, "Swan Lake."

Although classical performance was one of his favorite things, the last thing Jim felt like doing at the moment was to sit through a ballet production.

He felt tense and pressured, and would have preferred to spend his time trying to work out a plan to present to Eric the next day. He calculated quickly; dinner, one and a half hours; ballet, three hours; coffee and dessert following the ballet, another hour. Then the drive and the possibility of getting tied up in traffic. Jim estimated the evening would cost him at least six hours. Six hours he could spend working on coming up with a plan that would give his boss some level of hope.

What he felt like saying to Jill was totally different than what he said. "Sure, honey, I'll be on time. See you at the restaurant at six."

"Great," Jill sang. "Happy birthday, darling."

"You already said that," Jim found himself chuckling over his wife's doting.

"I'm shooting for 36 times before the day ends," she laughed. "I love you."

"I love you too," Jim's voice softened. "You have no idea how much. See you at six."

As Jim placed the handset back in the receiver, his mind returned to the problems at hand. He had no way of knowing that this day would turn out to be more than a great birthday, it would be one of the best days of his career.

♪

Jim and Jill sat in the concert hall waiting for the performance to begin. Their front-row seats allowed him a good view of the symphony orchestra preparing in the orchestra pit. His mind wondered as he watched the musicians tune their instruments and warm up for the production. Some were practicing parts of the music that was about to ensue, while others sat quietly still, ready to begin. When Jill gave him the envelope with the performance tickets, she told him that she had contemplated buying tickets for a production of Mozart scheduled for a couple of days later. Instead, she decided on the ballet because this was an internationally acclaimed symphony orchestra.

The squelching, non-uniformed noise emanating from the practicing musicians was anything but pleasant to Jim. He wondered how a group of world-class musicians could produce such unappealing sounds when they weren't playing in unison. His thoughts again turned to how he might have spent this time more wisely by staying in his office working out a strategy for tomorrow's pivotal meeting.

The noise continued, bringing Jim's attention back to the orchestra. He watched the performers intently, thinking about how interesting it was that when left to their own devices, they produce only a less than optimal sound. But when they work in unison, the resulting music so beautiful that it inspires people to pay large amounts of money and travel great distances to hear.

As the lights dimmed, a fast, measured silence ensued from the orchestra pit. Jim's attention turned back to the performance. A sudden outburst of melody nearly stunned him. It was hard to believe that the individual screeching from the instruments could so suddenly turn in to such phenomenally beautiful sound. The music continued as the curtain slowly raised, revealing the first scene of the performance, set in the garden surrounding the castle of Prince Siegfried.

Jill handed him a program. As he was tucking it into his suit pocket, Jim suddenly sat upright with the same feeling one gets when a forgotten name feels like it is sitting on the tip of the tongue. His gaze turned again to the orchestra. Just as one of the musicians turned a page of his music score, a sudden awareness came to him.

"That's it!" he said so loud that the man sitting to his left glared at him. My god, that's really it!" he said again, in near disbelief. The jab from Jill's elbow against his ribs didn't feel particularly good, but he ignored it. His mind began calculating, weighing, strategizing, all while onstage, Prince Siegfried's mother chastised her son and beseeched him to choose a bride during tomorrow's ball.

Jim's sudden awareness was about how the orchestra, a compilation of individuals playing different instruments could come together with such a concrete level of unison in order to create music of such beauty. He realized he had always known, but he had never applied it in this same manner. The musician turning the pages of his sheet music had elicited this epiphany. It struck Jim that sheet music was the world's oldest and most ingenious form of cross-functional process mapping imaginable. Each player knows exactly how to interact, when to interact and in what manner. The map tells them when to play, with what momentum, what notes to emphasize and even when to breathe.

As he thought about it more, Jim realized that every player must have a slightly different map, yet the system of maps yielded the desired result—the music necessary for the dancers on stage to follow. It was a perfect example of individual—and unique—processes within an organization all having the same ultimate outcome. He also realized that the way the players were measured and rewarded was based on their ability to follow the process map, or in the case of the musicians, the sheet music. Rewards came in the form of audience applause and peer and public reviews. The key measurement, of their success, however, was in the ability of the dancers to move to the music in a prescribed fashion.

The ballet had now reached act two before Jim was able to focus on the actual performance. The beauty of the swans gliding across the water, the music, the lighting and the entire theater atmosphere struck him. He leaned over and kissed Jill's cheek. "Thanks, sweetheart, I'm having a great time," he whispered. Jill smiled.

Act three of Swan Lake takes place in the ballroom of the castle. The master of ceremonies introduces six princesses. Looking at the master of ceremonies on stage made Jim once again think about his epiphany. Master of ceremonies, dancers, musicians, conductor… Conductor! What is the role of the conductor—he wondered.

Jim realized he had overlooked a critical player in the performance system he was watching unfold. He thought about how the conductor is usually the one person in a performance, particularly symphony performances, who receives the majority of the accolades. He thought about some of the celebrated conductors of our time; Kurt Masur, Leonard Bernstein, Herbert von Karajan and Sergiu Celibidache. But what is the conductor's exact role? He stared intently at the conductor in the pit, trying to look for clues. Jim noticed that one of the conductor's hands seemed to be keeping time, as though he were moving things along. He also appeared to send signals to various players, or groups of players. There seemed a particularly strong interplay between the conductor and one of the violinists. There were also prearranged events where the conductor would merely look at someone in a particular way and the musician understood his unspoken gesture.

As Jim was making these observations, another thought struck him—and he found himself dumbfounded by its simplicity and logic. The conductor is nothing more than a manager of people. His job is to get his organization to produce beautiful music, yet he does not play an instrument. The success of his organization, in this case, the orchestra, depends on his ability to make the people follow the process maps that have been clearly drawn and which they have access to at all times. To do this, the conductor must be able to clearly communicate his vision of how he wants the music to sound. Jim assumed that he probably works with the musicians, and groups of musicians, individually. For example, he probably works with the woodwinds, strings, percussion and other "teams" separately to establish acceptable performance standards or goals for each of their areas. Jim's enthusiasm continued to grow as his theory unfolded. His thoughts seemed to be lining up outside of his brain—just waiting for a pause in thought to jump in.

The ballet was in its pivotal scene. Prince Siegfried is conned into swearing eternal fidelity to the wrong princess. His decision culminates in the death of his real love, Odette, and himself in the lake during a storm.

That's not going to happen to me, Jim thought. For years, I thought I knew everything I needed to know about management—I was the golden boy and I could do no wrong. But the real problem is that I have been loyal to the wrong princess. There are better ways to do things—better ways to manage the people who work for me.

Jim had, in his mere enlightenment, committed himself to finding a better way. He felt more enthusiastic than he had in a long time. The light at the end of the tunnel was fully in his view.

♪

Over dessert and coffee following the performance, Jill looked at her husband with concern. "What's up Jim? You look like you just swallowed a canary. Are you okay?"

"Am I okay?" he responded with raised eyebrows as the waitress placed their piping hot cappuccinos in front of them. "I'm more than okay, honey. I haven't felt this great in a long time."

"I didn't realize you like ballet that much, honey. I didn't even think you were particularly excited about going tonight."

"The ballet certainly contributed to my elation, sweetie, but it was more than the performance that got me going. I can't say more about it right now, but I want you to do something for me."

"What?" Jill's furrowed brow revealed her confusion. Jim didn't reply. He had started writing something on a paper napkin.

"Remember that vacation you've been asking for?" Jim smiled. "Will you call the travel agent tomorrow and book a three-week trip to Bora Bora in November? I think I've found a way to make it happen."

Jill's smile grew into a wide grin. "You're the best!" she said as she stared down at what he had written:

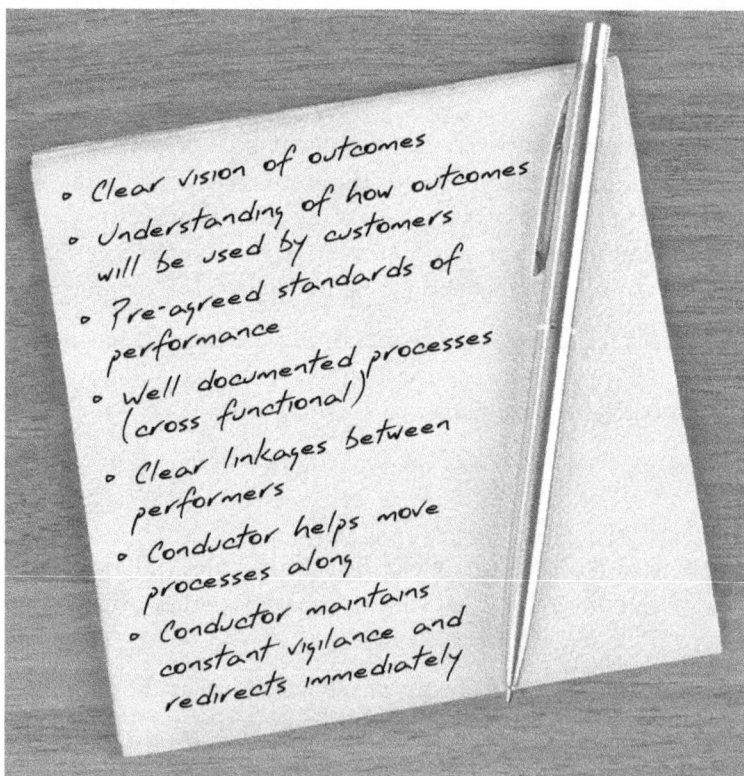

- Clear vision of outcomes
- Understanding of how outcomes will be used by customers
- Pre-agreed standards of performance
- Well documented processes (cross functional)
- Clear linkages between performers
- Conductor helps move processes along
- Conductor maintains constant vigilance and redirects immediately

It had been a birthday filled with great surprises, and a truly wonderful evening.

Chapter 2
Getting the Team On-Board

Jim woke at five the following morning, and for the first time in months, he did not have to drag himself out of bed. He quickly remembered that Jill had the alarm clock set 20 minutes ahead, feeling if he thought he was running a little late it would help him get out of bed faster. He never understood her reasoning, but he agreed that even under normal circumstances, he was not an early riser.

Within 40 minutes, he was showered, shaved and dressed. He bent down and gently kissed his still sleeping wife goodbye, knowing she still had another hour before she had to awaken to start her day.

Jim began formulating a plan for the day during his drive to the office. He braked suddenly for a caution light, spilling a drop of Starbucks coffee on the car seat. He reached for the napkin in his breast pocket, but quickly remembered that it contained his notes from the previous evening. He wiped up the coffee with a tissue instead. As he waited for the traffic light to change, he adjusted the earpiece of his cell-phone and began dialing his direct reports, leaving the same voicemail message for each of them:

"Make my office your first stop after you get this message this morning, and don't count on doing anything else until after four this afternoon."

It was still dark as he pulled into the parking space bearing his name. As had been his habit for years, and because he was usually the first executive to arrive at the office, he flicked the light switch on in his office, placed his briefcase next to his desk and headed for the lunchroom to turn on the coffee maker.

Jim's office was large and bright. Photos of Jill and the kids were neatly arranged on his desk. Scuba-diving pictures during Jill and his first trip to Bora Bora hung on the wall—near his Superior Managerial Performance Award. His glaze swept across the wall décor, bringing a slight smile to his lips. Adjacent to his desk was a small conference table with seating for six—just enough for his team members.

Larry Cummings, head of operations, was the first to arrive. By 7:30, everyone was there. Judi Grantham, Spencer's VP of finance, Sean McCoy, VP of human resources, Pete Brown, VP of sales and Gary (Bud) Snitzer, director of marketing, filed in one at a time and took places at the conference table. The entire team appeared somewhat puzzled over the sudden call from Jim to attend this morning's meeting.

"How was your meeting with Eric yesterday?" Judi asked as she adjusted herself in a chair.

"It's been rescheduled," Jim answered. "Pammy called at two and rescheduled it for this afternoon." He could hear Judi's deep breath.

"Whew," she verbalized, "I thought you called this meeting to tell us the bad news."

"No, this meeting is for an entirely different purpose," Jim answered as he took his traditional seat at the head of the table. "To be honest with you, I don't know where to begin here, so let me ask you guys a couple of questions. But first let me put things into some perspective."

"You all know that the purpose of the meeting with Eric this afternoon is for me to explain what we are going to do to improve the situation at Spencer. It's no secret that quality is down and sales have dropped. Although we've discussed this on numerous occasions, we haven't come up with satisfactory solutions." Jim paused as he glanced at the napkin he had placed on the table in front of him.

"Everyone involved with Spencer, employees, vendors and especially customers, should view it as a company where customers get products they have been involved in helping to design. Those products should be delivered in a timely manner—and without defects. Although I'm certain you already know this, I wanted to verbalize it again so there is no doubt as to my vision. Another fact all of us now sitting here know is that we're not accomplishing that vision—at least not currently.

Silence fell over the table—an unspoken acknowledgement that what Jim said was undisputable.

Larry Cummings broke the silence first. "Jim, you know I agree that quality has been the pits, but I also know that my people are working overtime trying to fix the problems. Just yesterday, I held a meeting with my production managers and supervisors to try to come up with solutions. As I've told you before, they all hold quality as a top goal, and know it is what they are rewarded on, but…"

"Let me stop you for a moment, Larry, and I'm sorry for interrupting," Jim said. "I know your division people are working flat out. But you bring a valuable point to surface. Why didn't you invite some of Judi's purchasing people and some of Pete's inside sales people to your meeting yesterday?"

Judi and Pete looked at Larry in unison for his response.

"We were trying to solve a production problem, Jim. "I didn't see the need to invite everyone in the organization. We all have enough meetings as it is. We just agreed that we have some good people in operations. I wanted to give them an opportunity to fix things."

Jim looked at Judi and Pete for their reaction. Pete spoke first. "Come to think of it, some of our customers don't need the same product quality as our more high-tech customers. Maybe some of what we're currently defining as poor quality really isn't poor in some customers' minds. Perhaps one of our sales people should be in your production meetings, Larry, so issues like this can be highlighted."

"Some of our purchasing agents might have interesting stories about raw material availability that could be of interest in a meeting like this," Judy injected.

All faces turned to Jim, anticipating his reaction. "Herein lies what I believe is the primary problem," he said. "Do we really know who should be involved in what, and when, around here? Are we overlooking some major improvement by this sort of siloing? If our mutual end goal is to satisfy our customers, what are the most critical things, as an organization, must we do on a systematic and regular basis to accomplish that? I certainly don't have the answers. I don't know that anyone in this organization has them. Frankly, I find that frightening. What appears to be happening is that we all work our backsides off, but only to maximize our own areas of influence— rather than the customer's total experience. Sometimes we overlook the consequences of not linking properly with other areas. Am I wrong here?"

"Jim, I agree with you," Gary spoke for the first time. "It sometimes feels like each of us are running our own little businesses within the organization, yet we have no choice. None of us is a Mother Theresa model."

All eyes rested on Gary until Jim responded. "What do you mean, you have no choice?"

"It's what we get paid to do, Jim," Gary said. "We get paid to run our own businesses. I'm sure Pete's compensation is based on sales. Larry's is based on what he produces. Mine is based on my ability to design and implement the marketing programs. Remember the old adage that says you get what you pay for? I think it's fair to say that people do, and are measured on, what they are rewarded for."

"You're right," Sean offered. "And the result is that we perpetuate the same philosophy with our people. Let's face it, we measure them on the same things we're measured on!"

Jim took the ensuing brief silence to peer at the napkin again. "I think we're getting somewhere," he said. "Essentially, you are saying that we are going to have to reevaluate our expectations and performance standards to ensure they are in alignment with what customers want. But I think there is more to it. Let me ask you the same question I asked a moment ago, but a little differently: what are this organization's five or ten most critical processes?"

Jim's question caused Judi's memory to flash back to a book she had recently read on process improvement. "I can tell you some of mine," she responded. "There is the invoicing process, payables process, check reconciliation process, monthly salary process, purchasing process, credit check process…"

Sean interrupted. "You're right, Judi. Those, I'm sure, are some of your important processes. But are they necessarily Spencer's most important?"

"Exactly!" Jim exclaimed. "We all have our opinions regarding the organization's most important processes, but I don't think those opinions are unanimously shared among us—at least not currently.

"I want to share an experience with you," Jim took a deep breath, emphasizing his call for everyone's attention. "Jill and I went to a production of Swan Lake…" He went on to recount the story of the epiphany he had the previous evening. As his story drew to its end, the team members were dumbfounded. Jim sat quietly, watching their faces as they contemplated its meaning.

"That's a really interesting way of looking at it, Jim," Larry finally spoke. "And it makes so much sense! If we could agree on a set of overall goals for Spencer, define the critical processes and how they relate with one another, make sure that everyone is reading from the same piece of sheet music, so to speak, and if we, as a management team, can put in place a set of metrics that allow us to maintain constant vigilance, yet avoid having us play everyone's instrument for them, we can finally get our hands around producing some products that are high quality."

"Particularly if we get customers involved, up front, in a more systematic manner," Gary added.

"This is exciting," Judi smiled at her boss.

"That's exactly how I felt last night," Jim also smiled. "I'm glad you sense the same potential here. Still, we have to come up with something for my meeting with Eric today. We are not going to be able to accomplish this process in just a few days, and unfortunately, companies are managed on short-term performance. This fact may buy us some time, but we have to come up with a valid and solid plan of how we're going to attack this issue. Imagine what his reaction will be if I go to him this afternoon and tell him that we're going to start managing Spencer like an orchestra." His statement incited laughter that also acted as a brief stress-reliever. "I need a commitment from all of you," he continued. "Are you all dedicated to this idea?"

A combination of positive responses reverberated across the table.

"Let me get a flip-chart," Sean eagerly suggested. "I think more clearly when I have something to write on."

"Take a 15-minute break," Jim ordered. "Refill your coffee cups, check your e-mail, return important phone calls and get back here as soon as you can. He turned to Pete, adding "Would you please get someone to order in lunch for us?"

"No problem Jim, I'll get Hannah to take care of it."

♪

It was already 12 o'clock when they reconvened. Jim had written down a list of things he wanted to accomplish before his meeting with Eric in the afternoon.

"We need to come up with a succinct statement of what we believe is the problem or the critical business issue at Spencer," Jim set the meeting in motion. "It's vital that we agree on this first, otherwise we could potentially find ourselves attacking this issue from totally different perspectives, end up trying to solve different problems and wasting time. Although we haven't done any detailed analysis at this point, let's at least get a working definition. Next, it is critical that we deal with what we're going to do about the problem, in both the short- and long-term."

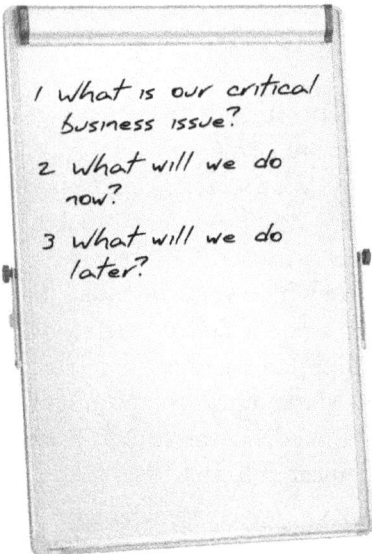

> 1 What is our critical business issue?
> 2 What will we do now?
> 3 What will we do later?

Everyone watched and studied the words.

"Based on the conversation we had before the break, I'd like to take a stab at defining the problem," Larry offered. "Think of the problem as something that is not happening, but that we would like to have happen in the organization. We are losing sales to better performing competitors because of quality problems. Also, our prices might be a bit high. I see several things contributing to these two problems. We don't have a sound handle on who should be doing what and when. That causes significant rework, missed hand-offs and general frustration. I also think we've done a poor job of clearly defining our expectations of people from this cross-functional perspective. Finally, somehow we're not measuring performance the right way."

"What do you think about Larry's statement?" Jim addressed the rest of the group. "Is that an accurate summation of our predicament?"

Everyone agreed to use Larry's statement as a working problem definition.

"Okay," Jim agreed. "Now, what are we going to do about it?"

"Let's go back to your example of the symphony orchestra yesterday," Gary suggested. "While I'm not certain about exactly how an orchestra works, it seems that one of the first things a conductor would do when preparing a new piece is to procure the appropriate sheet music. I'm assuming a copy is distributed to every musician. One set is for the percussionists, one for the strings, the woodwinds and so on. Assuming the conductor is the only one with the music for all sections of the orchestra. If I'm the conductor, I would need to understand what the sections will play, then I could give directions based on my expectations of each."

"Can I build on that?" Judi asked, but didn't wait for a response. "One of the first things we must do is determine exactly what the processes are, at least the processes that directly impact customer satisfaction. That's what the sheet music really represents, right? Once we know those processes, we should then conduct an analysis to determine their health.

"It's interesting," she added. "I now see where the book I read on process improvement falls short. That book is geared toward understanding what to do with a process, once you have it identified. It does not, however, take into account the linkages between the organization's important processes—and that's a key issue. How else do you know that you are spending the organization's improvement resources on the right things?"

"Hey, if it's going to define the organization's most critical processes, let's call that the 'Mission Critical List,'" Gary suggested, demonstrating his marketing expertise. "Then we'll do some analysis to determine which ones are most seriously broken. Then the next step will be to identify a couple of those processes and do some detailed redesign work on them."

"Sounds good to me," Pete responded. "The trick, however, will be how to do it. To be honest, I'm not even sure where to begin."

"Back up a step," Jim interrupted. "Let's focus on the what before we get to the how. I agree, there are many unanswered questions, but I feel sure we can sort them out later. Let's agree on what it is we need to do first."

"Consider this," Larry said. "The first thing we need to do is to agree on a set of specific goals for this effort. Specifically what do we want to accomplish? Once the answer to that question is in place, it will be critical for us to develop some kind of systematic measurement routine. I think everyone agrees that we have in place right now is much too haphazard. Finally, I think we're going to have to come up with something to satisfy Eric's requirement for short-term results. What we're describing here will require a little time to implement. Perhaps, during the analysis, we should be on the lookout for five or six quick improvement opportunities—something that can show Eric, employees and shareholders that what we're doing is producing tangible results."

"Larry, you're on a roll," Jim laughed. "You've made a great point about the short-term wins. This is something we really have to focus on. One word of caution, however—we must avoid letting these quick wins create overall piecemeal solutions. We need to accomplish both short- and long-term solutions, but at the same time. Larry is right. The best time to develop the quick hits would be during the analysis phase."

"Let me throw something into the mix, if I may," Sean interjected. "I'm not sure how to put this, but I think one of the most important things we can do is to take these changes 'down' into the organization as far as possible. Unless we can define exactly how job descriptions might change as a result of the improved processes, we'll be missing the point. Roles and responsibilities, it seems, will play an important part in this."

"Like the violinists who play under the lead violinist, right?" Judi chuckled.

"Exactly right," Jim said, just as a knock on the door drew everyone's attention. Hannah, Jim's assistant, announced that lunch had arrived. He turned back to his team. "We're making great progress, gang. Let's break for a bit of lunch. As we're dining, I'll try to summarize where we are on the flip chart. After lunch, we can add to, or refine it. Save a Diet Coke for me, please."

Deli sandwiches neatly arranged in clear plastic containers with a dollop of potato salad in one corner, and individual packets of Heinz mustard in another, passed around the table.

"I wonder why they put potato salad in these boxes," Larry joked as he opened a can of Sprite. "I've never seen anyone actually eat that stuff."

"When we got takeout food at my last job, it also came in these containers," Judi laughed. "Now that I think about it, it was the same kind of food. I think they're called 'clamshells,' which always makes me think they should hold some kind of a gourmet seafood meal— but it's always the same roast beef, tuna salad, corned beef or chicken salad sandwich. I visualize this giant takeout lunch manufacturing facility somewhere in the country's heartland. Every day, thousands of trucks drive in all directions across the country—from coast to coast—distributing these things. I wonder how much uneaten potato salad is out there on a daily basis. It must be tons—enough to keep half of the potato farmers in Idaho busy."

Everyone laughed. The mood in the room had changed considerably over the past few hours. Most of Jim's team members had expected the worst after receiving his voice-mail message that morning. But for the first time in a long time, they felt they were making progress as a unified team.

While they were eating, Jim stood at the flip-chart writing:

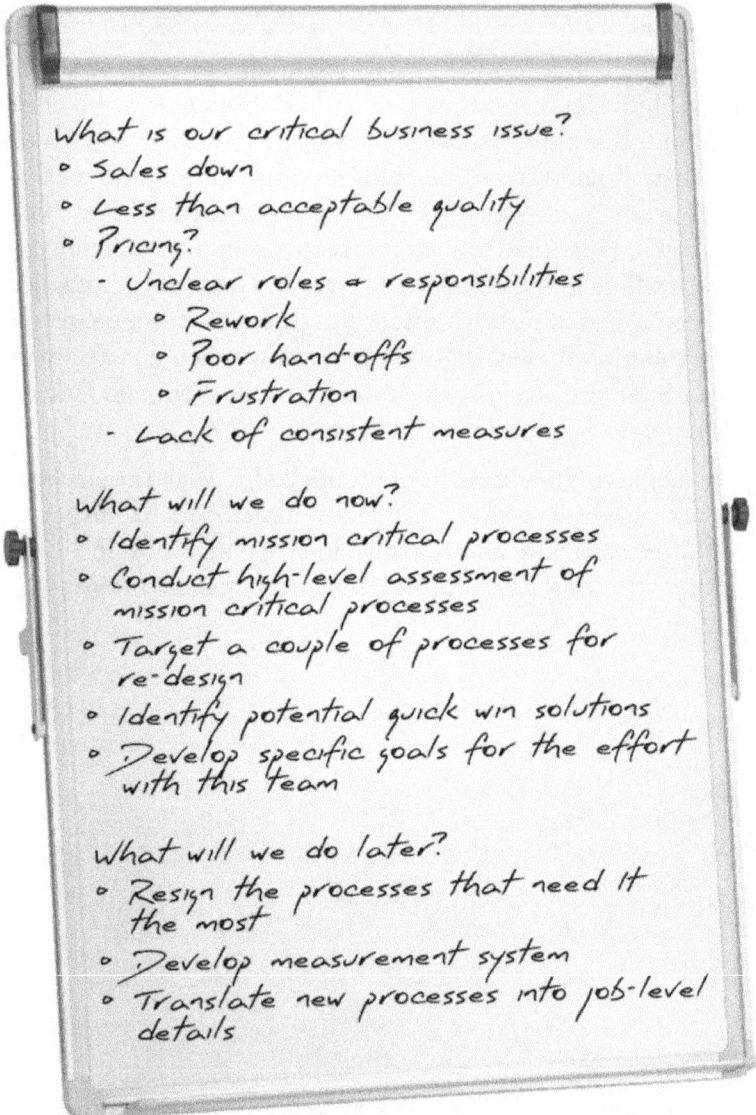

What is our critical business issue?
- Sales down
- Less than acceptable quality
- Pricing?
  - Unclear roles + responsibilities
    - Rework
    - Poor hand-offs
    - Frustration
  - Lack of consistent measures

What will we do now?
- Identify mission critical processes
- Conduct high-level assessment of mission critical processes
- Target a couple of processes for re-design
- Identify potential quick win solutions
- Develop specific goals for the effort with this team

What will we do later?
- Resign the processes that need it the most
- Develop measurement system
- Translate new processes into job-level details

Here's what we have so far," Jim said as the others were clearing the table. "Does anyone have anything to add? I'd like to finish this part of the discussion in the next hour or so." He glanced at his watch. "It's already 1:30. I'd like to spend some time discussing how we're going to do this before my meeting with Eric."

The team studied the flip chart carefully. "I think we're missing an important piece," Judi offered. "Something few organizations have a good handle on—implementation."

"You're absolutely right, Judi," Sean agreed. "Implementation will be the most critical part of this entire process. It's also somewhat related to the issue of sponsorship or ownership. Who will be the process owners?"

"That brings another good point to mind, Sean," Pete nodded. "It's something you hear people talk a lot about, but I, for one, don't know what it's supposed to mean. What do process owners really do? I think we're going to need a clear definition.

"Jim, as we're sitting here talking about this stuff, I find myself wondering about the how," Pete continued. "I know you said we shouldn't worry too much about it right now, but my concern is that when you present this stuff to Eric, he's going to want to know how."

"We've made significant progress already," Jim responded. "Perhaps now is the time to start talking about the how." He turned back to the flip chart and added the issues of implementation and sponsorship as he spoke. "I don't think we can be too specific at this point, because there's a lot out there we don't know yet. We'll inevitably learn many things throughout the process. How would any of you approach this?"

"We will definitely need to develop a project plan at some point, but I'm not sure we know all the necessary specifics yet," Larry said. "I suggest the most appropriate way to proceed is to form a team of people who know what they're talking about. This group should include the organization's stars, at both middle levels and from the front lines. A team made up of the right composition will be able to help us on the work that is needed on the front lines."

"I think we have enough for now," Jim said. "You're right, Larry. We're going to need a project plan, and we have to bring the right people together to form a team. Perhaps the best way for me to prepare for this afternoon's meeting is to convert some of these thoughts into a few PowerPoint slides. It will enable Eric to form a mental outline of what we need to accomplish in the coming months. Provided we have his blessing, we can spend the coming days as a team, flushing out the details on how to proceed. What do you think?"

Everyone agreed it was a viable plan.

As the members of Jim's team began to leave his office, Sean lingered behind for a moment. "Thanks for setting this in motion," he said. "Working on these issues together will create a much stronger team at the helm of this organization. I feel sure that strength will be transferred to the lower levels as well. If there is anything additional I can do to help, please let me know."

"I appreciate it Sean," Jim smiled warmly. "I'm quite excited to get going with this myself. Let's hope Eric shares our enthusiasm."

Chapter 3
Executive Buy-In

At five minutes to four, Jim gathered his notes and started walking down the corridor towards Eric's office, located in an opposite corner of the building, but on the same floor.

He stepped inside the reception area. A woman about 55 clicked away at her computer keyboard, unknowing of the intrusion. He leaned down and whispered, "Hi, Pammy," in her ear, causing her to jolt upright.

"You rascal," she smiled. "I should have known—Jim Robertson is never late for a meeting. It's good to see you. Eric is on a call right now, but he shouldn't be long."

"Nice to see you too, Pammy, although I can't wait for this meeting to be over."

"I am sure you'll do just fine, my boy."

Jim didn't mind her reference. He'd always considered her his adoptive workplace mother. The respect and admiration between them was mutual.

"He's off the phone," she said as she looked at the buttons on her telephone. "Let me see if he's ready for you. She stood, opened the inner door to Eric's office and stuck her head inside. Eric didn't wait for her to announce Jim.

"Send Jim in, Pammy."

She nodded and turned to Jim. "In you go, and good luck," she whispered.

As Jim entered the huge office, Eric stood behind his large, antique desk to greet him, a wide grin on his face.

"Let's sit over here," Eric gestured to the conference table at the other side of the room. "Sorry to have to reschedule the meeting at such short notice."

"No problem, Eric. It gave me a little more time to work on some solutions with my team."

"Good, and before we begin, I just want to reinforce how highly I value you and your team, Jim. Let's face it though, the results at Spencer, while by no means disastrous, have started to deteriorate. I know you also realize it. That's why I called this meeting. I feel I need to understand what your plans are to try to get things back on an upswing. There's no doubt in my mind about you guys being on the ball. This meeting is just to clue me in."

"That's exactly how I read it too, Eric," Jim replied. "And I appreciate your confidence. Of course, there is no disputing the early alarm bells, and they're ringing rather loudly. I've been very concerned of late. I've also spent a great deal of time and mental energy trying to figure out a way to turn this around as early in the game as possible.

"Let me start by telling you what we believe the problem to be, along with a few of the root causes," Jim continued. "After that, I'll share our thoughts about some fundamental changes we feel are needed. They have much to do with how we work together at Spencer, so they focus on internal cultural changes. But I think I've come with a potential and viable solution. I'm not here just to acknowledge the problems, Eric."

Eric responded with a nod, knowing Jim had more to say.

"I want to show you a plan; one that is very high-level at this early stage. It needs more flushing out, but I think it's important that you understand it and offer your approval before we move forward. I would also like to hear your opinion on the cultural issues we have identified. I think you'll find it interesting, hopefully even intriguing. If you agree with the principle, I'll gather my team together immediately to work out something more detailed. It's important that we're all on the same track right from the outset."

"Sounds good to me Jim," Eric responded.

"Let me explain it to you first, then I'll give you a PowerPoint presentation that will lay out the groundwork we've put together."

Jim leaned forward, his body language suggesting he wanted to be certain Eric followed his every word. "Sales are under significant pressure, and we believe there are two major reasons. We can attribute one to the quality problems we're currently experiencing.

The other is that our prices might be a tad too high in the current market environment."

"What makes you come to that conclusion, Jim?" Eric's eyebrows shot to attention.

"Several reasons," Jim answered. "Regarding sales, external competitive factors always have an impact, but we're beginning to think the primary reason for the declining sales figures has to do with our inability to produce good quality products. As we spent some time this morning discussing why, we realized the poor quality might have a lot to do with the way we, as a management team, have been running the organization."

Eric's expression told Jim his boss was puzzled.

"People in our organization are measured and rewarded on how well they optimize the performance of their individual areas of responsibility," Jim explained. "But when you really think about it, the job of satisfying our customers' needs occurs in several cross-functional processes. While customer satisfaction is a cross-functional activity, we have chosen to manage the organization functionally—not cross-functionally. We're failing because of the way we manage the organization."

Eric took Jim's pause. "This is one of the reasons why I have such great confidence in you and in your team, Jim. Many managers in your situation would have been looking far and wide for reasons as to why sales are falling or quality is down. They would focus their attention on all sorts of excuses, like the competition is playing with us unfairly, our raw materials are not up to par, we don't get the funding we need, the people we need or the skills we need to do the job. As always, Jim, you've put the onus squarely on your own and on the shoulders of the team you lead. I'm impressed. I like what you're saying about the way you're managing the organization. In fact, I wouldn't be surprised to find similar situations exist within most of our other operating companies. If you guys can crack the nut on this one, I'm sure some of the other companies could use your help. So, what's the plan?"

"It's critical that we focus on both a short-term and a long-term solution," Jim explained. "Without at least some short-term fixes, I realize there may not be a future. But at the same time, the solution we're laying will require some time to implement and take full effect."

Eric maintained his expression of intense interest, allowing Jim to continue. "Do you like going to the symphony?"

A puzzled expression returned to Eric's face.

"Don't worry, Eric," Jim chuckled, "I haven't gone off the deep-end."

Jim proceeded to tell Eric how the idea of the symphony plan surfaced, his meeting with his team earlier that day and the initial plan they had laid out. By the end of his explanation, Eric was held in rapt attention.

"Well, what do you think so far?" Jim asked, testing Eric's temperature.

Eric rubbed his chin, body language that Jim learned long ago meant his boss was contemplating.

It was a moment later before Eric spoke. "Frankly Jim, initially I couldn't make the connection between a symphony and organizational problems, but I'm beginning to see the similarities. Still, I need more information before I'm fully convinced. How are you going to get the organization to operate symphonically?"

"We have already agreed on the critical issues, Eric; failing quality and poor sales. Next, we need to understand the processes that have a critical impact on these issues. For example, I think there's a system of processes that impact quality the most. In our case, the processes with the highest impacts are planning, product development, raw material sourcing, production and shipping.

"Using the symphony example, you can see how this equates to the major orchestra sections, like the brass, violin, percussion, woodwind and so forth," he continued. "Once we know the mission-critical processes that relate to the business issues we're dealing with, we need to determine the health of each one. Our team agrees that one of the major problems we face is that we do not clearly understand the processes. It's fair to say that there are probably almost as many versions of each process as there are people in the organization. The processes have never been properly documented, and superior performance is often a result of superhuman effort—as opposed to a systematic way of doing business.

"Once we understand the health of each process, we can identify the ones that need 'fine-tuning,' if you'll pardon the pun," Jim's enthusiasm showed in the verbal roll he was riding. "The major improvement, however, will occur when we initially map the processes. Merely understanding what the major steps are, and who is involved in them, will make a huge difference in our people. It's just like the individual sections in a symphony orchestra understanding exactly what and how to play their instruments in a production. Sheet music is only a cross-functional process map. Without it, there's little likelihood that the same score would sound the same in the year 2010 as it did when it was created in the 1700s. The interesting fact is that the conductor is the only person with all the maps on one sheet."

"I'm beginning to get the picture, Jim. This process will enable you to clearly identify people's roles and responsibilities based on the desired outcomes for the organization—as opposed to functionally—which I'm sure is the current state of affairs. You might be on to something here."

"That's not all, Eric. It gets even better. Once we have the right processes mapped out, we'll develop individual goals and objectives based on the processes. This will enable us to take a close look at how people are being rewarded for what they do. Finally, we're going to have to develop an entirely new way of managing performance in the organization. Review meetings will be developed to measure and report on performance as it is related to the processes. One of the critical reasons why we're currently failing, I believe, is because we measure and report on the wrong things. Workers' accountabilities and rewards are in misalignment with the requirements of the processes." Jim paused to take a breath.

"You've got me," Eric smiled. "I'm in. But I have some concerns. This is going to take some time to implement, and we need to begin showing results quickly. I'm also worried that the process of creating the improvement itself is going to zap the organization of resources and divert focus for the short term. How do you propose to deal with those issues?"

Jim chose his words carefully, knowing that his response would be critical to get Eric's full buy-in. "I understand your concerns precisely, and I totally agree. As I said before, the plan has both a short- and a long-term step. My team and I discussed this very issue today. We propose to identify six to eight quick-wins for the firm during the analysis phase. We've already identified a few things that can help. We won't wait for the analysis, process mapping or redesign to take place before we pull the trigger on these improvements. Initiating a few less major things will provide significant results, and quickly. They will also help fuel the momentum for the change.

"On the matter of zapping the organization of resources during the effort itself, you're right again. Most of us have been involved in reengineering efforts like TQM, Six Sigma or other systems that required hordes of people to sequester themselves for days on end. They then emerge in a disheveled state with very little to show for their time or energies. Frankly, I think that's why most major organizational change is met with resistance and distrust. They offer little hope for success. We've all 'been there and done that' before. I don't have a complete answer for you yet, but I'm acutely aware of the problem. Be assured that I'll make every effort to insure that mapping and design do not become energy zapping 'flavor-of-the-day' efforts. I visualize a small and dedicated team that does a lot of the work offline. Then larger groups of people can validate the findings and designs. Small, quick moving and dedicated teams can do a lot. The tendency with other programs and systems is that they usually want everyone involved in every process. That won't happen here." Jim made a mental note to push his team on this issue as he paused for Eric's response.

Eric smiled. "Jim, my dad always told me that you were a great dancer. I know he was referring to the firm's holiday parties I didn't know that you're also an outstanding maestro. It's apparent that your heart is in the right place on this, and I am going to give you a pass. But you're going to have to do a little more planning with your people to convince me that we'll see the short-term results we need, or that the organization will not be unduly burdened by this effort. I like what I'm hearing, so go and put together a project plan. Let me know how I can help, or if there are funding issues involved. We'll need to discuss that too."

Eric looked at his watch. "Jim, I have a conference call in five minutes, so we're going to have to end this meeting. You have my go-ahead with the provisions I've given you. Get back to me in a couple of weeks and let me know how you're progressing."

♪

Jim returned to his office and nearly collapsed into his chair. He felt like he'd just come down from an adrenaline rush from eating too much candy. The feeling made him reflect on how excited his kids would get when they were headed to Disney World. At the end of the day they were so exhausted that Jim would have to carry them out of the park on his shoulders.

The meeting with Eric had gone even better than Jim had hoped. He and his team had Eric's blessing to implement Symphony at Spencer.

♪

Executive Buy-In

Chapter 4
What Makes a Symphony Orchestra Successful?

Contemplating the Symphony concept on his way to work the next morning, Eric realized he needed to add more meat on his plan. He knew it was important to learn precisely what combination of factors contribute to a flawlessly run symphony performance. His next task was to find out how from the right source. He remembered the evening of his epiphany—the sounds, the concert hall, the musicians, the conductor and even the audience's response. It immediately came to him that he needed to go to those who know exactly what it takes to make a concert successful. But he also realized the real evaluators of a symphonic performance is the audience." He decided to try to make appointments with a conductor, a couple of musicians and to try to find some audience members to gather some individual opinions on what they most appreciate in a performance. In these conversations, he hoped to uncover most of the keys to a successful symphony.

Reaching his desk, he immediately pulled out a notepad and his pen and began sketching an outline.

The first key to a successful performance is the written music, he thought. Even with the best performers in the world, the performance would still be average, or even bad, without a great music score. He decided it was the most important factor, so marked "Music Score" as "A."

Music by the classic masters, he considered, is never negatively influenced by time. On the contrary, the most famous scores by history's highest acclaimed composers are performed continually around the world throughout decades and centuries. And they are frequently used by today's performers from all levels of music—even rock and rap.

♪

In *Why Classical Music Still Matters* (University of California Press, 2007), Lawrence Kramer stated that classical music continues to matter because of its complex relationship with individual human drives and larger social needs. Eric had time to only skim the book before meeting with Sergei Sjostawinski. He noted, however, that success of a business project would be driven by the same elements.

"And it's obviously also because the music was written down that it has survived from generation to generation," Sergei spoke to Eric in slow and deliberate words.

Eric listened intently, but with an edge of disbelief that he was sitting with one of the foremost conductors in the world, listening to him talk about his art of passion.

"What can you tell me about the importance of sheet music?" asked Eric.

"Without it, there would be neither coherent or cohesive music," Sergei replied. "The sheet music describes exactly what the orchestra members must play, and how and when they must play. Think of it as a process map. If one performer doesn't follow the sheet music, the symphony falls to pieces. It's not different than surgeons and nurses involved in an intense medical operation, or the people involved— from the mechanic to the pilot—in an airplane flight. Details must be followed in a precise manner, and if even one person behaves in a way that is in conflict with the process, the consequences can range from a poor performance to a major disaster."

Eric was making notes as they were talking. He drew two circles:

In the outer circle he wrote "Sheet Music." In the inner, he wrote "Music," indicating the written piece of music as the center of success, and the sheet music as the second most important element.

Sergei continued, "Another critical element in a successful performance is obviously the quality and capabilities of the orchestra. There are outstanding orchestras and some that are mediocre at best. "And when you think about it, an orchestra is really just a collection of individuals who play together. My job is to keep them playing together as a team. The job of each performer is first to be skillful at playing his or her instrument, but they must also be willing to participate as part of a team."

"So what would you say determines the skill of a player?"

"Several elements," the conductor gave the question several seconds of thought before responding. "The natural skill the performer is born with, as well as his fundamental training in his or her instrument. But secondly, and almost as important, is practice. A good performer practices for hours every day, whether they are learning a new piece of music or trying to perfect a particular skill with which they need to improve. A conscientious performer will continuously try to improve."

"I see," Eric acknowledged, taking a moment to insure his next question was clear. "So what are the implications of this for the person who is leading the symphony orchestra?"

"First of all, if you are not aware, some major symphony orchestras have a unique hiring process. When players audition for an orchestra, they often do so behind a screen. This is so the hiring committee can focus only on what really matters—the person's ability to play—not his race, gender, religious affiliation age or other visual factors. Hiring is based purely on capability, and nothing else. Secondly, It means that the orchestra must provide ample opportunity for the performer to rehearse, whether it is rehearsal facilities or specialized rooms. And, it is imperative that orchestra members are provided with ample time for practice and rehearsal."

Eric was already beginning to assess what all of this would mean for his company in energy and effort, but he instead tried to focus on the conductor's monologue.

"Tell me," Eric asked, "when you get a group of talented individuals together like that, how do you make them work as a team? I imagine there would be a certain tendency for some of the performers to act as prima donnas, perhaps exercising their own egos or attempting to overpower other performers, isn't there?

The conductor smiled coyly. The thing you have to realize is that people do not come to a symphony orchestra performance to hear the individual performers play. They come to hear the orchestra perform and listen to the music. They come to hear one sound, the sound of the orchestra. Granted, the sound of the orchestra is the sum of the sounds of the individual players, but it is the collective sound that matters.

The conductor mused before continuing. "Sometimes we will have soloist playing in a particular piece. But in that case, it is specifically called for within the music score. "Something else you may want to consider is that there are music pieces in which some of the orchestra members play only a small piece of music. But they still must dress in coat and tails or another outfit ordered by the conductor and the producer of the performance. They must also get on a transportation bus or airplane, be in the symphony hall at a specific time, and be present for the entire performance.

"For example, he continued, "In Franz Liszt's Piano Concerto No. 1, it is used as a solo instrument in the third movement, giving the concerto the nickname of 'triangle concerto.' Were it not for that triangle player, the concerto would loose much of its magic.

If the triangle player overwhelmed the score by repetitiously playing the instrument, it would change the entire meaning of the score. Each of the players fully understand the context in which they are performing. And each fully understands the importance of what they are doing as a part of the whole, and they know what the conductor is seeking as the end result. And finally it is because they follow the process that has been laid out in terms of sheet music to the point."

But what role do you play in keeping them focused on working as a team?" asked Eric. "In the organizational sense, I have immediate access to information," Sergei replied without hesitation. I suppose many managers don't. The very second the players in the orchestra strike a note, I know what it sounds like. And if something has to be louder or softer, or slower or faster, I signal to the individual players and they make immediate changes to how they play the notes. I also know precisely at what point the performance is at on the sheet music at every second. If a particularly difficult passage is approaching, I can warn the relevant players in advance by providing them with a pre-assigned signal. Interestingly enough, I do not get involved in playing any of the instruments myself. If I did, I don't think I could be as effective as I am at conducting the performance.

As Eric was perched on every word the conductor said, his mind was also quickly assimilating how an orchestra's performance was perfectly applicable to his organization and its team's functions. Management Information in his company was notoriously slow; monthly at best. The majority of the team leaders and managers spend a great deal of their time doing the work that the people they are managing are supposed to be doing. He realized it is impossible for the managers to have time to manage because they are too busy doing the manual work. Eric glanced at his watch, surprised that he had taken so much of the conductor's time, despite that Sergei seemed intrigued and interested in Eric's theory that an organization team could function efficiently by using an orchestra's performance culture as an example.

"Sir, this has been an eye-opening conversation," Eric stood, extending his hand. So much of what you have told me is applicable to my own company. You have helped me to understand the reason why some of our functions are either failing or not as efficient as we plan." "I have merely shared with you what I do every day, but I am glad if I've been of some help," Sergei said as he stood and reached for Eric's hand. I do have one suggestion, Eric, "speak to one or two of the members of the orchestra before you leave. Perhaps you can also gain some insights from them."

♪

Before leaving the building, Eric made appointments with two of the orchestra performers for the next day. He wanted some time to reflect on what he had learned from his conversation with Sergei, and he wanted to clean up his notes so he could be better prepared to ask specific questions during the meetings.

Back in his office, he opened his notebook portfolio and wrote:

- The quality of the music is the most critical factor—the score is typically a masterpiece or has a melody that is pleasing to the audience

- Accurately written sheet music is the second most critical factor

- Performers must be proficient in their instruments, and experienced enough to understand precisely how a concert functions and what their individual role in the concert is

- Performers must practice relentlessly

- All performers work from the same sheet of music

- Performers receive constant direction by the conductor

- The conductor receives immediate, real-time information and makes instant decisions regarding changes

- Performers all have an important role to play, no matter how much or how little time they spend playing their instrument

- Performers must function as a team every moment

- The audience is interested in the sound of the symphony, not the sound of the individual performers—the only exception are solo performances

- The performers all understand how they impact the whole, and they work towards one common goal at all times

- Performers are hired or fired, based on their ability to play, not because of gender, race, race, religion or other forms of discrimination

- The conductor does not play an instrument during the performance—he remains 100-percent focused on managing the sound of the performers

♪

Eric reread his notes several times. He was certain the list could be adapted to his organization's situation, but he was far from proclaiming it final. He felt sure his conversations with the performers the next day would add even more valuable advice.

♪

Eric arrived at the symphony building at 8:30 the next morning to meet with Sylvia Meinberger, one of the orchestra's violinists. As he entered, he could hear the music coming from the various practice rooms. He met Sylvia in the room number where she had instructed him to meet her. Mr. Sjostawinski explained a bit of your quest to me yesterday," she smiled as they shook hands. "You want to know what the key factors are in a successful concert."

Eric took a seat at the gesture of Sylvia's hand. She meticulously placed her violin in its case on an adjacent table, and then sat in a chair facing him.

"Yes. Exactly. But he said it may be beneficial to also speak to a couple of musicians to get a perspective from another viewpoint. He recommended I speak to you and a couple others. "There is no great secret here," Sylvia responded, her warm smile still illuminating her pale skin. "Successful musicians, and consequently a perfect performance, are the result of early training and rigorous training. Our instruments, of course, are integral to that success."

"Your tools-of-the-trade, so to speak," Eric interjected.

"Precisely. Have you heard the stories about musicians buying first class airline seats just for their instruments?"

Eric smiled and nodded.

"If you play a Stradivarius, for example, it makes perfect sense. But regardless of the value of the instrument, as musicians we are worthless without them. The instrument is integral to every musician, and not only in classical music. B.B. King named his guitar Lucille. Eric Clapton's most famous guitar is called Blackie. Our instruments are an extension of the musician, and it takes on its own personality. I think it is the same for famous chefs. They hoard their knives, forbidding anyone else in the kitchen to touch them. A mechanic chooses his tools with tremendous concentration. A writer's primary tool is the computer, and each is chosen by how it feels, performs and reacts to what its user demands of it. It's the same in every industry. And not only is it important to choose the right instrument, but it is imperative that it is cared for in way that reflects its value."

"Yes, I see your point," Eric agreed.

"Clarinet players often cut new reeds for mouth pieces themselves to ensure they are the perfect form and size. Viola players are known to polish their instruments to a perfect reflective shine. Through this process of caretaking, developing an intimate relationship with the instrument is inevitable. You get to know the tool and how it will— and will not—react to what you ask of it.

The thought occurred to Eric about the connection between people who love their work, and those who work because they must. He wondered if how a tool is cared for had a connection. He stored the thought in the back of his mind, resolving to think more about the point later. "Do you ever want to improvise on a piece of music," he asked. "I mean, is your own personal creativity ever reflected in how you play?"

"Of course that urge occurs. But if I want to improvise, I'll take an evening off and go to play with a jazz band in a club. Or sit in my own living room composing music. But if I want to be a part of a symphony orchestra, I must be willing and able to play exactly what is expected of me. It is as though Mozart or Brahms wrote the music, and the composer, conductor and the score has a total grip on you throughout the piece. And the minute you step out of line, the conductor is there to snap you right back on track."

"Can you tell me more about the conductor's role? If dozens of conductors are using the same music, shouldn't all of their concerts sound the same?"

"The conductor is the single most important key to a successful performance," Sylvia mused, "It's interesting to note how some conductors become world famous, while others do not, yet they play the same music." "As I said, it's the conductor's job to ensure that all the musicians in his orchestra stick to the script at all times. More importantly, however, it is conductor's responsibility to anticipate difficult passages and lead the musicians through them to ensure we are playing the right rhythm. And the most important aspect is his it's his ability to communicate with us. He communicates what to stop doing, anticipated difficulties, keeping our speed in check, our velocity in tune and so much more. He keeps us working as a team. The conductor's ability to communicate makes the real difference in a symphony."

Eric considered her words, taking a brief pause to collect his thoughts. Then, "We have talked about training and practice, the instruments, the role of the conductor and other things," said Eric. "I really appreciate your time, and I know you must get back to your practice, but is there anything else that comes to mind that you feel is important?"

Now Sylvia paused for a moment. "This may sound fairly straight forward, and might go without saying, but the quality of the microphones, and more importantly, the acoustics of the concert hall can have a huge impact on the quality of our output. I suppose in an office environment, the work environment and layout would be the corresponding factors."

As Eric reflected on her words, he realized that environment and layout was one of those things that might often be discussed at Spencer, but it would rarely change. It always seemed too difficult to quantify the potential benefit of the types of changes that have to do with workplace environment.

♪

Later that day at his desk, Eric sat began to organize his notes from the conversation with Sylvia, adding to the list he had worked on following his conversation with Sergei Sjostawinski.

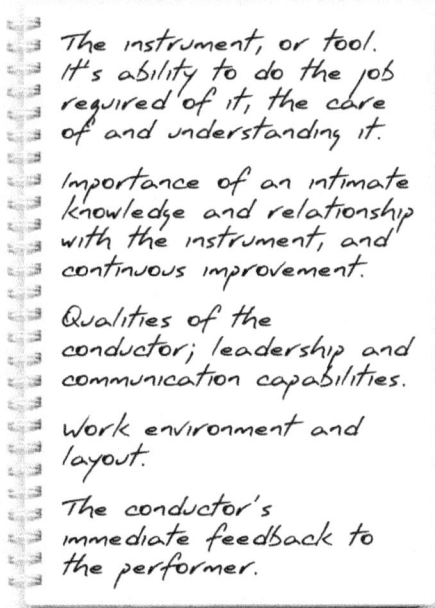

The instrument, or tool. It's ability to do the job required of it, the care of and understanding it.

Importance of an intimate knowledge and relationship with the instrument, and continuous improvement.

Qualities of the conductor; leadership and communication capabilities.

Work environment and layout.

The conductor's immediate feedback to the performer.

Chapter 5
What is a Symphonic Organization?

Jim reflected on his journey of the past two weeks. It was only a short while ago when he had been sitting at his desk wondering how to change the course of his organization because things were doing downhill. Since then, he had attended that pivotal performance of the symphony orchestra, rallied his team and created excitement about the Symphony concept, had gained his boss' approval, met with the conductor and a musician from the orchestra. The knowledge he had amassed in two short weeks enabled him to understand what it takes to successfully deliver superior orchestral performance. But where to next?

Jim was acutely aware that a change of the magnitude presented by the symphony concept was not going to be something that he could do alone. He decided to call another meeting with his top team to see if they could help flush out what he had learned from his recent conversations about successful symphonies. His goal was to essentially create a model for how an organization that is managed, similar to the critical elements that make a symphony work.

In preparation for the meeting with his team, Jim prepared a couple of flip charts with headings, using his notes from the previous day's conversations.

When his team arrived and settled into their seats around the conference table, Jim noticed that they too seemed to change. An air of excitement fell over the meeting room. The team members were eager to hear from Jim. They wanted to know how the meeting with Eric had gone, as well as what he had learned from his subsequent conversations with the members of the symphony orchestra.

Jim made his presentation using the outline he created from his notes. The meeting became heated at moments as questions were flying through the air. But he took each one and dissected it in order to make them all understand. They kept at it for hours with only momentary breaks. Jim ordered a tray of sandwiches and beverages, and they ate together as they talked. By the end of the day, the team had agreed on a list that compared the functions of a symphony orchestra and that of an organization that is managed in a similar fashion.

♪

A Symphony Orchestra	A Symphony Organization
The quality of the music score itself is the most critical aspect of a symphony. It is typically considered a classical masterpiece, and one that the audience is familiar with or is pleasing to the ear.	Products and services must be superior, beyond equal and tailored specifically to customers' needs and wants. To accomplish this, a highly intimate knowledge of the customer is required.
Sheet music is the second most critical element. All musicians and/or performers must work from the same sheet of music, following it verbatim line by line.	Processes are clearly defined, updated and communicated. Staff and team members follow the process precisely as it is written. Each member understands exactly how their performance affects the performance of others and of the goal at hand.
Performers are all experts in their fields.	People must be supremely fit for their roles. The recruiting process is critical. A skills evaluation of all existing employees measured against the roles they are playing is critical in insuring that the right people are in the right positions.
Performers practice relentlessly	A significant amount of time is devoted and multiple resources are used in training and re-training team members.
Performers receive constant feedback and direction from the conductor. The conductor receives immediate/real-time information on which to base timely decision making.	The leaders of the organization must receive constant real-time information about performance. Any off-schedule conditions are immediately communicated to job performers who in turn take immediate action. Without frequent information the leader is powerless to lead, and instead is left to watch the performance occur without his or her guidance and leadership.

A Symphony Orchestra	A Symphony Organization
Performance expectations are very clear through not only the sheet music, but also through practice sessions during which the music is rehearsed and re-rehearsed in groups or individually under the close supervision of the conductor and team leaders.	Expectations of employees are precise and clear. It is necessary for each employee to articulate exactly what success looks like. Staff and team members must understand clearly what constitutes outstanding, mediocre and poor performance.
It is imperative that musicians have an intimate knowledge of and relationship with their instruments. They strive to care for and improve on them continuously.	Staff and team members are required to have an intimate understanding of the tools needed to do their jobs. Technology and systems are continuously refined to continue catering to customer's needs.
The audience is interested in the sound of the orchestra combined to result in a symphony, not in the sound of individual performers, unless there is a soloist.	Customers are interested in the service or product outcome, and they want their overall experience to be as positive as possible. Customers are not interested in the internal workings of the organization or why something is not possible. Customers want the best possible service and/or product in the quickest possible time at the lowest possible price. Customers do not care who in the organization takes care of them or their issues, they care about expedient and efficient resolution to every issue they have. Customers want convenience, efficiency and one-stop shopping.

A Symphony Orchestra	A Symphony Organization
Musicians and performers all have an integral role, regardless of how large or how small. Therefore all musicians and the conductor will demonstrate mutual respect to one another. The goal of individual participants in a symphony orchestra is to produce a flawless score, which is the optimal collective. No one will strive for an individual sound. The performers all understand how they impact the whole and are working towards one common goal at all times.	All job performers are equally important to the goal at hand. All receive equal respect. Participating staff and team members are all very clear and accepting of the importance of each of their own roles on the overall realm of the task. This, in turn, renders them more concerned about the quality of their individual work. Performers understand that teamwork is necessary for the achievement of the ultimate desired outcome. Employees' goals are team-based where possible, and explained to supervision when not. Interoffice politics are frowned upon. Promotions and advancements are based entirely upon performance, and not an ability to manage stakeholders. Teams of employees are involved in major hiring decisions, and teams of employees are involved in major firing decisions. Boundaries and silos are less prevalent than in other organizations.
Immediate feedback to the performer from the conductor is imperative at all times.	Employees should instinctively know if they have performed poorly, mediocre or superior. Team leaders must provide direct feedback. The consequences of performance should be immediate and tightly linked to the overall expectations of each employee and the ultimate goal of the combined team.

A Symphony Orchestra	A Symphony Organization
Performers are hired or fired based on their ability to play, not because of gender, race, race, religion or other discriminations.	Employees are hired and/or fired based on their capabilities as measured by the job requirement. Each is evaluated entirely on performance, not on gender, race, age, religion, sex or other discrimination. All staff and team members are treated with mutual respect.
The conductor does not play an instrument during performances. He or she remains 100-percent focused on managing the sound of the musicians.	Managers and team leaders do not engage in the actual manual work that the people on their teams are paid to do. Managers and team leaders spend 100-percent of their time managing the people in their groups with the goal of obtaining the best possible performance and the highest goal. A broader span of organization control may be required as one-on-one and one to four-on-one reporting relationships may be inadequate to insure the most productive use of a manager or team leader's time.
Work environment and layout is critical to the overall sound of the orchestra, as well as to musicians' comfort and desire to be in attendance.	The layout in the organization should be closely linked to the design of the key processes. This will avoid unnecessary hand-offs and wasted time of varying kinds. In a proper work environment, process turnaround times will improve and costs of production will reduce. The work environment should be conducive to employees working.

A Symphony Orchestra	A Symphony Organization
Instruments are critical to a superior performance and therefore the best that money can buy. Instruments are cared for daily.	Technology and systems must be in total support of the job performers as they carry out their roles.
Conductors are not all the same. Two keys to superior Conductor performance are his/her leadership and communication qualities and capabilities.	The team leader is key to the performance of the organization. His or her ability to lead, to anticipate and to direct as performance occurs is critical to the performance of the organization and the outcome of the goal. Leaders' ability to communicate can often make the difference between success and failure. Leaders are sometimes put into leadership positions without the proper leadership training, often because they have continuously exhibited extraordinary technical capabilities in their previous roles. A critical review of leadership training requirements should be taken on an ongoing basis, and investment in development of leadership skills is critical.

♪

When he felt the list was as complete and concise as possible, Jim emailed it to a clerical assistant at her desk adjacent to the conference room, asking her to print enough copies for everyone in the room. Silence hung over the team as they all studied the list. Larry Cummings, vice president of operations stood and walked to the light-switch and turned on the fluorescents hanging over the table. Jim glanced out the large picture window and realized dusk was settling in on the day.

A few non-conspicuous yawns ensued. Larry spoke as he settled back into his seat at the table.

"This is not information that we all don't already know," he offered, breaking the silence and causing everyone to shift into more conscious posture. "These points—or functions, if you will—are the sound basics of running any business. Get the right people to do the job, tell them what their job function and goals are, give them the tools to accomplish those goals, instruct they should function within the team, inspire them to work as a team member and let them know when they are doing a good job. Or, a bad job if that's the case. It is really quite simple!"

"You're right," Sean McCoy, head of human resources concurred. "But this is different in that we all already, intuitively, this is what needs to happen. In this raises a question in my mind; if we all know what needs to happen, why isn't it happening on a systematic, regular and comprehensive basis?"

"Simply because we tend to loose sight of the overall picture when much of our time is devoted to crisis management and firefighting," injected Bud Snitzer, head of the marketing department. "Frankly, we tend to get involved in solving pieces of this list, not the entire list as a whole. If someone is not performing in his or her job capacity, we either fire them and hire someone we feel is better qualified and able, or train and retrain them. Either of which is highly expensive. Yet because we do not provide the staff member with frequent feedback about their performance, they may not be aware of what is factually expected of them. The processes may not be appropriately or clearly understood by the person. And then sometimes we engage the organization in projects of various kinds. For example, we may train everyone, or initiate "the latest-greatest-reengineering project.

Peter Brown, head of the sales department interjected, "But the problem is that these projects tend to become isolated events. And we never take a step back to look at the whole picture. What is accomplished, for example, to train and retrain people if we are not going to change a broken process? Or, give people a task, but without the proper tools to accomplish it? Beyond being effective for a short period of time, it likely doesn't help at all, and the failure process has been an expensive one for the company. Someone once said that if you put a good performer in a bad system, the system will win every time[1]."

"I can't speak for the rest of you, but I really want to do this, offered Judy Grantham, chief financial officer. "I want our organization to work like a symphony orchestra. "But how do we actually operationalize this process? How do we execute it?"

Jim let the conversation flow back and forth across the table for several more minutes. He wanted as much feedback as possible from his group, but he also knew it was imperative to understand how the Symphony process emotionally resonated with the group. Finally, he took the floor.

"Okay everyone, your input and your feelings about this program will be a sizeable change for Spencer. And besides being inevitable, change can carve a path for positive growth and re-growth. Fortunately, I don't think any of our employees would object to this team managing the organization like a symphony orchestra." "But I do think we have to use caution and sensitivity in how we communicate the process to our staff. If we are going to be successful in this endeavor, people must view it as a positive step forward. It is imperative that staff members do not become fearful for their jobs, or threatened with a drastic operational change. Would anyone like to take a stab at proposing how to move this forward?"

"I'll take a stab," offered Judi. "Give me a day or two and I'll come back to this table with something in hand."

Her offer pleased Jim. He realized it was important to get their team's buy-in, and the only way to do that was to get them intimately involved in the process from the beginning. Without total team involvement and constant communication between members, the Symphony process would probably not be a successful endeavor.

The Team agreed to meet later in the week to discuss Judi's proposal for how to implement Symphony.

---

[1] **Geary Rummler, Ph.D.**, a visionary management consultant with expertise in the application of instructional and performance technologies to organizations. Geary founded or co-founded several leading consulting firms; Praxis Corporation in the 1960s' The Rummler-Brache Group in the 1970s, and; Performance Design Lab in 2000. Geary passed away October 29, 2008 but his partners at Performance Design Lab continue to honor his legacy.

Chapter 6
Implementing Symphony

As she walked toward her office, Judi considered the best approach to get the new Symphony concept implemented.

This is a major project, she thought, and the changes must be communicated to the staff appropriately so as not to induce fear.

She decided to first focus on what precisely the change would be. She reflected on the notes, now tucked into the portfolio under her arm, remembering the double circle Jim had created.

A basis for a model, she thought.

She reached her desk, gently pushed aside the messages and notes her assistant had left for her before leaving for the day, and pulled a notebook from her drawer. Maybe I can use this as a basis for a model she mused as she began scribbling. After several moments of concentrating on the page in front of her, she stared at the model.

Success of a Symphony

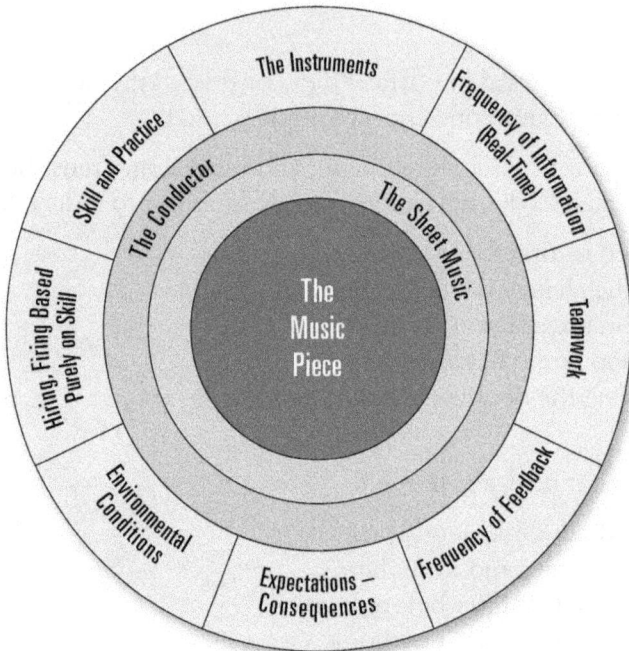

Satisfied it was a fair depiction of what Jim had learned in his conversations with the members of the symphony orchestra, and a sound assessment of what the team had discussed in today's meeting, she laid her pen on top of the pad, crossed her arms and sat back staring at what she had just created. But it suddenly occurred to her that it was important to determine what a symphonic business organization model looks like on paper. She recalled the conversations in the meeting about the organizational implications of how a performance is organized and run. She picked up her pen and flipped the notepad to a blank page.

Symphonic Organization

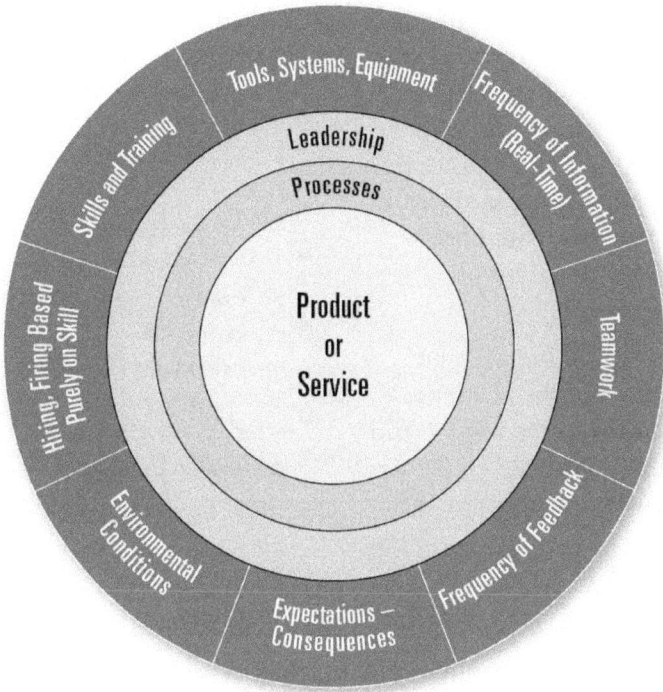

Staring at the model when she finished, she realized it was similar to the model she had drawn for the orchestra.

I guess the devil is going to be in the detail, she thought. "I need to add more meat to the bone so people will know precisely what we are talking about.

Judi placed the notepad and her portfolio containing the notes from today's meeting in her briefcase. She thumbed through the notes and messages left on her desk. Feeling secure that no details had fallen through the cracks with her in the meeting all day, she took her briefcase and headed home for the night.

♪

Studying the notes again as she was winding down after dinner, Judi decided to try to operationalize the thoughts the team had as a total entity at the meeting. Using the model she had just developed as a basis, she jotted down some notes on the notepad, and decided that in the morning she would break the elements down into a specific list.

As she reviewed her list, she noticed most of the elements were captured in the model, and that several additional elements were in further support of the model.

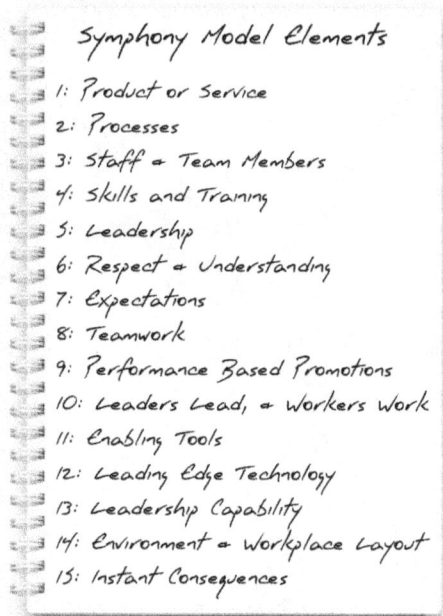

Symphony Model Elements

1: *Product or Service*
2: *Processes*
3: *Staff & Team Members*
4: *Skills and Training*
5: *Leadership*
6: *Respect & Understanding*
7: *Expectations*
8: *Teamwork*
9: *Performance Based Promotions*
10: *Leaders Lead, & Workers Work*
11: *Enabling Tools*
12: *Leading Edge Technology*
13: *Leadership Capability*
14: *Environment & Workplace Layout*
15: *Instant Consequences*

Element 1 – Product or Service

Product or Service

Without exception, products and services must be superior in quality and maintain competitive advantages over those of comparable value and price. Products and services must be tailored specifically to customers' needs and wants. This requires an intimate knowledge of the business culture, functions, operations and preferences of our clients.

Procedure:

• Continuous market research and development of "killer-app" products

• Continuous Test and Learn programs/Innovation

• Maintaining product and service value propositions strong enough to create price insensitivity

• Service in a class of its own (e.g. Singapore Airlines)

• Large continuous pipeline of new product development

- Clearly defined market feedback loops from frontline to research and development staff

- Maintaining an intimate knowledge of customers in order to clearly define their needs and wants

Element 2 – Processes

Processes are clearly defined, updated and communicated on a continual basis. Employees follow the process precisely as it is written. Each team member comprehends clearly how their performance affects the performance of others.

Procedure:

- Documentation of processes

- Streamlining mission critical processes

- Removal of any and all waste (LEAN, etc.)

- Process audits to ensure compliance

- End-to-end process training

- Process metrics and KPIs (Key Performance Indicators)

- Goals are process-based; not silo-based

Element 3 – Staff and Team Members

Staff and team members must be supremely fit for their roles, therefore the recruiting process is critical. A skills evaluation of all existing employees versus the roles they are assigned is critical to ensuring the right people are in roles that fit their level of overall ability.

Procedure:

- Skill assessments for each task

- Assess and continually update recruiting processes

- Company university (in-house training programs)
- Certification for key frontline roles
- Certification requirements for each task performed
- Annual and/or bi-annual re-certification and retraining

Element 4 – Skills and Training

Skills and Training

Significant amount of time and resources are devoted to training and re-training of employees.

Procedure:

- Company university
- Induction training
- Technical skills straining
- Certification programs
- Yearly re-certification
- Every employee has a personal development plan which is being monitored

Element 5 – Leadership

Leadership

Leaders are powerless to lead without frequent information, and are left to merely observe performance. This results in unacceptable conditions. Leaders of the organization are required to receive constant "real-time" information about performance. Any off-schedule conditions are immediately communicated to job performers whose task it is to take immediate action.

Procedure:

- Relay task and/or function performance information in a real-time/desktop-access manner

- Task and/or function performance is relayed as expediently as possible

- Performance is frequently reviewed, with intervals dependent upon the task and assigned deadline

- Action is signed out immediately

- Action is followed up on a frequent pre-set schedule

- Employees "own" the information

- Employees know their performance level grade at all times during the task/function

Element 6 – Respect and Understanding

All job performers receive equal respect, and share an equal level of importance to the accomplished goal. Performers are all cognizant of the importance of their individual role and its impact on the overall function and result. This ensures their individual concern of the quality of their work.

Performers understand that teamwork is necessary for the achievement of ultimate desired outcomes. Employees' goals are team-based where possible.

Interoffice politics are frowned upon. Participants reported participating in such activity will be dealt with on an individual basis.

Promotions and advancement is based entirely upon performance, and not an ability to manage stakeholders.

Teams of employees are involved in major hiring and major firing decisions. Boundaries and silos are less prevalent than in other organizations.

Procedure:

- Staff and team member diversity and inclusion

- Acknowledgement for performance is rewarded in bonuses

- Firing for poor performance is institutionalized

- Performance outcomes are not dependent on how much time is spent at work, or the ability to be good at stakeholder management

- Processes are clearly defined and communicated to ensure that all members understand their roles and part of overall goal

- Teams of employees are involved in major hiring decisions

- Teams of employees are involved in major firing decisions

- Boundaries and silos are less prevalent than other organizations

- Metrics are process-centric and not silo-centric

- Rewards are process centric and not silo-centric

Element 7 – Expectations

Expectations – Consequences

Expectations of employees are concise and clarity is acknowledged. Every staff and team member must be able to articulate exactly what is his or her vision of success. Employees must have no doubt what constitutes good performance or poor performance. Functioning in a way contrary to these expectations is continuously measured.

Procedure:

- An in-place rigorous goals translation process

- The goals' process is tied to the annual budgeting and quarterly forecasting processes where such exist in the organization

- A System For Managing is in place that rigorously measures the performance against agreed upon objectives

- Performance against objectives is frequently monitored and noted on a pre-set weekly, daily or hourly schedule

- When off-schedule conditions are uncovered, immediate action is taken to rectify the situation

Element 8 – Teamwork

Teamwork

Customers are interested in the service or product outcome. They want their overall experience and final outcome to be beyond their expectations. Customers are not interested in the internal workings of the organization, nor in being told why something is impossible. Customers want the best possible service and/or product in the most expedient manner and for the lowest possible price. Customers do not care who in the organization takes care of them or their issues. Rather, they care about resolution to every issue that surfaces. Customers want one-stop shopping.

Procedure:

• Processes are designed to produce minimum turnaround times

• Processes are as **lean** as possible

• Processes are designed based on customer feedback

Element 9 – Performance Based Promotions

Employees are hired and/or fired based on the capabilities required to do the job. Staff member evaluations are based entirely on performance, not gender, race, age, religion or sex. Employees are treated with respect at all times and under all circumstances.

Procedure:

• Diversity and inclusion

• Financial compensation for performance

• Institutionalized job dismissal for poor performance

• Performance outcomes are not judged on the amount of time staff and team members spend on the job, nor on stakeholder management

Element 10 – Leaders Lead, and Workers Work

Managers and team leaders do not engage in actual manual work that is the responsibility of their staffs and team members. Managers or team-leaders spend 100-percent of their time managing the people in their groups and overseeing the tasks at hand in an effort to obtain the best possible performance and goal outcome.

This element will require a broad span of control in the organization. One-on-one to four-on-one reporting relationships may not ensure the best use of a manager's time.

Procedure:

• Span of control minimum five

• Formal Leadership training

• Leadership goals focus on team performance

• Leadership goals do not focus on individual performance

Element 11 – Enabling Tools

Technology and systems will be in total support of the job performers as they carry out their roles.

Procedure:

• No manual workarounds

• Complete technology audits

• Turnaround time of IT (information technology)/systems department

• Systems flexibility

Element 12 – Leading Edge Technology

Employees are required to have an intimate understanding of the function of the tools they need to do their jobs efficiently and thoroughly. Technology and systems are updated continually, and are continuously updated and refined to continue catering to customer's changing needs.

Procedure:

• IT research and environmental scanning

• Continuous IT and systems testing

Element 13 – Leadership Capability

The manager or team leader is key to the performance of the organization. His or her ability to lead, ability to anticipate and to direct as performance occurs is critical to the performance of the organization. Managers and leaders must be proficient at communication in order for staff and team members to understand clearly their tasks.

Leaders are sometimes assigned to leadership positions without proper leadership training. This can occur when a leader continuously exhibits extraordinary technical capabilities in their previous roles.

A critical review of leadership training requirements should be taken on an ongoing basis. Investment in development of leadership skills is critical.

Procedure:

• Leaders have the necessary skills to lead

• Leadership training programs are continuously provided

• A good leader is not necessarily the best technician, nor is the best technical necessarily a good leader, re; a top sales manager is not necessarily the best salesperson

Element 14 – Environment and Workplace Layout

Environmental
Conditions

The layout in the organization should be closely linked to the design of key processes in order to eliminate the risk of unnecessary and varying types of hand-offs and wasted time.

Process turnaround times will improve and costs of production will reduce.

Evaluation and renovation of the workplace environment is periodically conducted to insure it is conducive to employees working efficiently and expediently.

Procedure:

• Layout makes logical sense and follows the flow of work

• Working environment is clean, organized and conducive to work

• Layout follows process and is conducive to teamwork

Element 15 – Instant Consequences

Expectations –
Consequences

Employee training will include staff ability to immediately recognize if they have functioned at their task in a positive or poor manner.

It is incumbent upon the leader to provide direct feedback.

The consequences of performance should be immediate and tightly linked to the overall expectation of each employee.

Procedure:

• System for managing

• Immediate feedback

Judi read and reread her list. Finally feeling that her eyes needed a break, she sat back in her chair and took a deep breath.

Effectively, this gives us a better view of what it means to be a symphonic organization, but now what? Now what? How do we implement this? Virtual pages of thoughts were flipping through her brain. She thought back to the many previous experiences with organizational change she was involved in during her career, and the glitches and challenges that came with each one.

She realized that the most effective efforts in implementing change in her experience had a few factors in common. They almost always seemed to follow some type of clearly outlined methodology. They also had some type of an assessment phase, a specific design phase, an implementation schedule and a phase where the achievement of the results were monitored and corrections were made where needed.

Judi picked her pen up from the desk pad and started jotting again.

Implementing a Note-by-Note Symphonic Organization

Step 1 – Assessment of Current State:

- Using the Symphony wheel model (or 15 element list derived from the model) as a comparison basis, assess how well the organization currently performs

- Identify all possible existing gaps

- Determine potential alternatives to close all possible gaps

Step 2 – Design of System Following Change Implementations:

- Evaluate the design alternatives that have been identified during the assessment phase

- Based on the evaluation, create solid designs for every element that does not conform to expectations

- Create a strategic implementation strategy

- Create a precise implementation plan

Step 3 – Implementation:

- Based on the high-level implementation strategy and implementation plan, further develop a detailed implementation plan

- Assign appropriate implementation resourcing

- Initiate implementation

Step 4 – Monitor:

- Monitor implementation rigorously at scheduled intervals

- Revise implementation plan as appropriate

♪

The team met the following day to review Judi's outlines and suggestions. Time allowed for reading the list, followed by a brief question and answer period, the group expressed concurring and overwhelming acknowledgement of the superb job Judi did at putting the details together for the Symphony model. Effectively, she had developed not only the model, but also created an implementation process that was clear and concise. The team agreed the model would likely require modification during the implementation phase, as issues were expected to surface that could cause kinks. All unanimously agreed that they were committed, and prepared to initiate the project without delay.

Jim smiled. He was delighted that the team had aligned themselves around both the concept, and their willingness to begin the implementation process immediately. The energy and eagerness in the group was high, and starting without delay would mean that everyone would bring their enthusiasm to the project. He anticipated a smooth implementation process. "Let's start at the beginning," Jim leaned into the table for everyone's attention. "How are we going to staff this project? How should we involve ourselves in the process?

"My initial concerns are that we are the only people in the company who know what the Symphony concept is and how important it will be for our company," he continued. "How do we get our people to buy into the concept? How can we maintain the ability to provide oversight that ensures that once they are in it deeply, it doesn't evolve into some anarchistic new approach to doing business as Spencer?

A short pause of silence followed as the team considered Jim's questions. Larry spoke first. "I have read somewhere that about 70-percent of these types of organizational change efforts fail. And they fail for numerous reasons. Sometimes, for example, the right amount of attention is not dedicated to the project by the organization's top leaders. In some cases, failure is due to the organization not dedicating resources to the project."[2]

"Experts have stated that sometimes failure occurs when success is not measured," offered Sean. "And sometimes it is because the organization declares victory too soon.[3]

"There can be many other reasons," offered Judi. "I think we have to get a good view of exactly how this project would work before we dive in." "All good points," Jim injected. "We are essentially talking about two separate issues. First we need to determine the various team structures that should be in place. Then we need to determine how to manage the change aspects of this project. This would include a communications' plan and an involvement plan. Who will take the lead on these?"

Larry was the first to throw in his hat. The team agreed to meet again the next day to discuss Larry's change and stakeholder management plan.

---

[2] *Conquering Organizational Change: How to Succeed Where Most Companies Fail,* Pierre Mourier, Martin Smith, PhD, (CEP Press, 2001)

[3] *Leading Change; An Action Plan from the World's Foremost Expert on Business Leadership,* John P. Kotter, (Harvard Business School Press, 1996)

Chapter 7
Project and Change Management

Back in his office, Larry began formulating an outline of exactly how the project would work. He admitted to himself that he was slightly intimidated by the task at hand. He was highly experienced, and knew most organizational change efforts of the magnitude of the Symphony project commonly ended up as failures, or at the least such projects did not deliver the benefits initially expected.

He knew he had to address two key factors. He had to determine the ingredients for a successful project, and he had to uncover where to find those ingredients.

He began by trying to find out as much as he could by searching change management and project management on Amazon.com.

Solution after solution surfaced as he searched. He jotted down notes as he proceeded. Later that night at home, his search continued. At nearly midnight, as he stared at his notes, he recognized a number of traits he felt were important to build into the Symphony project for Spencer.

He woke before dawn the next morning, turned on his laptop, created a new document and titled it "Spencer's Symphony Change and Stakeholder Management Plan," and proceeded to outline the plan.

- Change must be central to the strategy

- Senior management and executives must be fully bought in

- Fulltime resources must be allocated to the project

- Continuous communication is essential on all levels

- Measure progress aggressively and frequently

- Involve broad organization

- Create key change champions

- Identify the meaning of victory precisely at the beginning of the project

- Avoid declaring victory until it meets the preset meaning.

- Create alliances in support of the change

- Ensure that all teams are working on the change every day

- Monitor key sponsors daily to ensure total alignment

♪

Larry paused to study his list. He realized it was not much different from the majority of the information he had gathered during his research. He considered what made his outline outstanding in comparison. As he continued to study his list he had a sudden epiphany that made him realize that the idea behind successful change implementation was, after all, quite simple.

♪

<hr>

Change Management and Project Management

- Make a decision, but understand completely why that decision was made

- Get the best possible people to work on the project on a fulltime basis

- Continuously measure the progress of the project

- Communicate on a preset schedule, and be accountable for all communication

- Be certain that you are bringing people along

- Avoid letting go too early

- Monitor regularly to ensure that everyone is on the same page throughout the project

- If you start it, finish it

♪

Larry paused to dissect each of the factors on the list. He started typing again.

Make a decision, but understand completely why that decision was made:

Intuitively, we may all feel that the decision being made is a great one, "but based on my experience from other projects, the going can get tough," he thought. Once that happens, if why the decision was made is vague, it is easy to let it go because it becomes too difficult to accomplish.

An understanding and unanimous agreement is necessary regarding what the results of the decision will mean for the organization as a whole, and for every person involved individually.

These must be measurable goals against which performance will be measured on a systematic basis. The goals must also be clearly communicated to the rest of the organization so every staff member will feel a harmonious and emotional connection to the project.

Get the best possible people to work on the project on a fulltime basis:

Larry realized that achieving this objective could be much more difficult than it could appear. Many projects are staffed by people who are not functioning in a specific role, and ultimately are assigned to a project in order to create a job function. Managers and executives are not likely to be willing to sacrifice their top performing people to guarantee the success of a project. But if there could be a system of warning or anticipation, the possibility would exist to back-fill positions vacated by the project people, and to create proper "hand-overs" to ensure continuity of the day-to-day work. He considered which of his colleagues were best suited for an oversight position of this type, and thought about the work Judi had done such a good job on.

He thought back to Judi's development of "Implementing a Note-by-Note Symphonic Organization." He listed the necessary skills that people must have in order to fill such positions.

Process Capability: Someone with a process methodology understanding to work on the elements of the project.

Subject Matter Experts: Besides process capability, these people must have some key technical (subject matter) expertise to ensure the processes designed are relevant and implementable.

Performance Management: People who understand performance management metrics and KPIs. Ideally, this person is resident in the finance or a similar department.

Systems and Technology: A critical role for the success of the project, these people must be capable of insuring that job performers have the right tools and information available. They must also oversee and confirm that processes are enabled by the right technology, and that performance management systems and metrics in place are as automated possible.

Human Resources: A successful result requires highly trained and experienced human resource personnel. Human resource staff are responsible for conducting skills' assessments, for frequent critical examination of staff members and to insure that all placements are monitored on a repetitive schedule. Job tasks also include compiling appropriate training plans and that routine trainings are in place. Additional tasks include insuring that all recruiting and/or job dismissals are appropriately and legally conducted.

Project Management: The complexity of the project requires staff members who are highly experienced in managing large projects. It is the responsibility of the project managers to remain engaged in the project from commencement to completion.

Frontline Staff: The Symphony process requires information from the frontline to coordinate with exactness the project design with the market for which the organization operates. Efficient involvement of these staff members will eliminate the possibility of "ivory-tower" mentality.

Continuously measure the progress of the project:

Larry contemplated how best to measure progress. Clearly, a measurement of adherence to whatever project plan is agreed upon is needed, and in the form of "adherence to milestone-type" metrics. Some type of measurement of adherence to the budget agreed upon for the project is also necessary. "Finally—and potentially most important—is the measurement of achievement of the agreed upon positive impacts to the organization. Once these impacts begin to materialize, they can be used to merchandise the success of the project to the rest of the organization, as well as other stakeholders.

Communicate on a preset schedule, and be accountable for all communication:

The issue of metrics brings us to communication, Larry thought. The achievement of performance improvements can be used for communicating success to the organization. But what other issues need to be communicated, and what is the most efficient way to communicate?"

He thought about the phases of a project and started writing a "what" and a "how" table:

Project Phase	Information to be Communicated	Communication Channel
Initial Phase	• Why are we doing this? • What will it accomplish? • How will the project work? • Process • Team members • How to provide suggestions • Employee's concerns (job security, role security	• Initial broad-based global email • Town hall style FAQ session • Internet site for extensive information with a "suggestion" link
Analysis	• What are the key findings? • What is the next step? • Merchandising of any quick-hit opportunities that are uncovered	• Intranet site • Global email • Poster boards in key departments • Hotlines and suggestion boxes • Formal presentation at the end of this phase to show findings and solicit input for the design • Meeting with key champions who are prospective leaders

Project Phase	Information to be Communicated	Communication Channel
Design	• Design plan • Key design areas • Reinforcement of jobs and roles • Solicitation of input • The final design • Any early successes achieved	• Internet site • Formal global broadcasts • Champions' meeting • Formal presentation of the final design • Targeted formal training programs, as required by the design
Implementation	• Schedule adherence • Impact measurement • Reconfirmation about jobs and roles • How things are changing • Champions of change; people who have excelled in their job functions • Implementation awards • Customer experience stories • Newspaper clippings • Company awards	• Intranet site • Regular global broadcasts • FAQ town hall sessions • Creation of a champions council
Monitoring	• Selected elements of above as needed	• Selected elements of above as needed

Be certain that you are bringing people along:

Regardless of how much leaders of organizations communicate and involve their people, it never seems to be enough. A leader whose goal is to create change of the magnitude required in order to reach the principles prescribed by "Symphony" must pay acute attention to insuring that key people in the organization are brought along throughout every step of the process.

Customers: Larry wondered if it was possible to incorporate actual customers into the process in order to canvass their opinion. If not, a method of acquiring customers' must be developed.

Avoid letting go too early:

Change experts estimate that approximately 70-percent of all change efforts fail.[4.]

A major reason for failure is distraction on the part of management. They often move onto something else too early in the process because the change effort faces challenges or appears too difficult. A primary key to implementing the "Symphony" process is to stick with it until results materialize.

Monitor regularly to ensure that everyone is on the same page throughout the project:

A tight system of measuring key successes is critical in order to for managers, team members and others involved with the Symphony program to realize the right level of benefits and to be able to market these benefits any and all critical stakeholders.

When the change is successful, it is important that key people know the results that the Symphony process is producing. Measuring frequently will enable mid-term corrections as they are needed.

If you start it, finish it:

Larry was thinking back to projects that he had undertaking in his past life with different other corporations. Priorities always seemed to change. If a project is well thought out and had been deemed a good idea on day one, why should that drastically change on day 60 or 90? – New information will come to light, but Larry remembered his frustration with a boss who continuously wanted to change the goal posts and conditions. "Once the goals for the project have been agreed," Larry wrote, "declare success when those goals are met and not before!"

♪

Larry again considered the ease with which it took to sit and write down the process and key points, but he expected that doing it would be significantly different. How could he be certain that those

---

[4]*Reengineering the Corporation - A Manifesto for Business Revolution*, Michael Hammer and James Champy, Collins Business Essentials, HarperBusiness, Rev. Upd edition (October 10, 2006)

involved would follow each process and step while rigorously attending to the detail of each? Unless he could figure out a way to make this part of the normal way for the organization to conduct its business—melding it into its culture—as opposed to doing things differently from the normal "business as usual routine there would be a high probability of failure. He knew he had to figure out a way that the process would become "what we do the "Spencer Way."

An organization is a structure; a way of doing things as a set of processes. Larry pondered this idea and came to the conclusion that the Symphony process had to be formalized in order to have it reflect Spencer's culture.

Larry came to the conclusion that Spencer needed a formal department to be responsible for the project. It would require a department head whose goals and objectives were his or her full-time job task. He then started wondering about cases or organizations that are good at translating strategy into action. Suddenly it came to him; what organization is better at developing strategy and then implementing that strategy relentlessly, despite what might sometimes seem like insurmountable odds against implementation. The answer was clear—the armed forces are superior in relentless implementation because they utilize generals who are trained in these capacities. He felt there was a good lesson to be learned from the great warlords of history.

We need a war room, Larry thought. A place where all the information about the Symphony project would be immediately accessible and where the top team members and managers could meet and make instant decisions about mid-course corrections when needed.

He envisioned the room; a place with graphs and hanging on the walls; a place where meetings would be held on a moment's notice when needed; where people who are responsible for the elements of the change would come and make presentations and report their progress throughout the process.

♪

Everyone on the same page through out the entire project:

The issue of keeping everyone on the same page throughout the project stemmed from the realization that different teams would be working on the project as it moves through its various phases. These various project teams must be kept in alignment, and so a way to develop vertical alignment throughout the layers of the organization was necessary.

On a previous occasion, Larry had experienced a project where the management team had led a project team loose on an issue in order to "empower" the team to use their creativity in designing the best possible solution from their vantage point. The team worked together for a month and returned to a result meeting with a solution that was totally unacceptable to their superiors. The project was never implemented, and the time, energy and money spent to develop the project was lost.

He started thinking about how he could successful depict the various teams and how they would interrelate and interact. He decided there would be four separate groups:

1. **A steering team** consisting of the CEO Jim, Larry and Jim's top direct reports.

2. **A project team** that would vary in membership depending on the particular phase of the project, but would represent the key full-time team. These team members would consist of bright and energetic members of the organization. They would be responsible for doing the majority of the analyzing, designing and implementation of Symphony into the organization.

3. **A Symphony team** representing the formal team whose sole job it would be to ensure that the project came to fruition. The members of this team would act as team facilitators, provide methodology for process improvement and KPI development, oversee the overall project management and track results. This team would also be responsible for change management and flawless communication to the rest of the organization regarding progress and successes. Finally, this team would act as a liaison between the project team and the steering team to ensure appropriate support from the top team and the CEO. Larry

believed that the best place for the leader of the symphony team to be reporting was to the CEO.

4. **Shareholders and other external groups** would represent the key interested parties who would receive and review regular updates on progress. This group of people would include the CEO of Spencer Services, Spencer's holding company and key stakeholders such as customers and regulators.

Larry sketched the team structure:

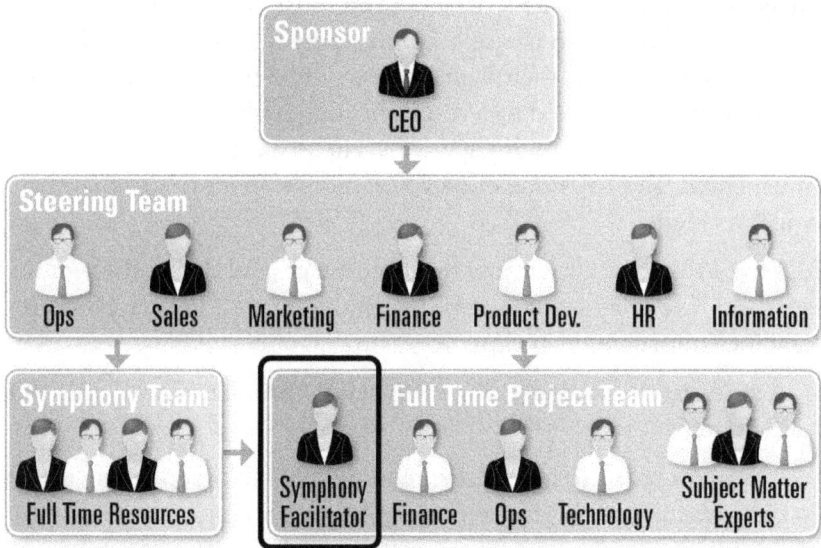

He summarized his thoughts, and reflected on what he had prepared for the meeting with Jim's top team.

Implementation and project management:

• Make a decision and understand why it was made

• Be clear about the objectives of the project, both in impact terms (financial) and in personal terms (what will this mean for those people who are involved)

• Get the best people on the project on a fulltime basis

• No tourists or people who are there for a "look-see"

• There must be "skin-in-the-game"

Measure Progress:

- Create metrics of success (impact) as well as milestone attainments and costs

- Use a war room to ensure the project takes center stage in everyone's minds at all times

Communication:

- Develop a formal communication plan for each phase of the project and work the plan relentlessly

- Do not let go of the project too early

- Keep everyone on the same page throughout the project

- Create a formal stakeholder management/team structure

- Maintain a review progress between steering and project teams at the end of every phase, or more frequently if needed

♪

Larry made his presentation to Jim and the top team. It went well, and they essentially agreed to Larry's proposal. They unanimously agreed on the importance of project management and of full-time capability on. They also agreed on the necessity of a full time symphony team, for the duration of the project at a minimum.

Jim contemplated which of the team members were most qualified to be in charge of the project on a full-time basis. It was also important that the chosen person could easily be freed of his or her daily duties.

But Jim caught himself in his thoughts. Finding the person who is easiest to free from their job tasks is precisely the mindset we have always had with new projects—and it was exactly what he had warned against in his presentation. He realized he would have to follow the same mindset in selecting the leader of the Symphony team, but it was more important that the chosen team leader was perfectly suited for the position—someone at the top of his or her game—even if that meant having to hire and train someone to assume the person's current role.

Jim had no doubts; he knew Larry was the best person to lead the effort. Larry was the head of operations, he understood project management and he had already offered his services. Although Judi was also a good candidate, she was not as strong at project management as Larry.

♪

"All right folks, let's take a quick break," Jim said to the team. "When we reconvene, I want us to decide on the next specific steps." As he left his office, Jim saw Larry standing at the water cooler. "Larry, do you have a minute?" he asked.

"Are you pleased with my presentation?" Larry asked as they walked toward Jim's office.

"I'm more than pleased," Jim answered as he patted Larry on the shoulder. "You did a great job … Jim closed his office door behind them, and immediately turned to Larry to complete his response … I want you lead this project—I want you to head up Symphony."

Larry paused for a minute to consider Jim's proposal.

"Wow, I am flattered, but what about operations? It's a full-time job, and it typically requires more than a 40-hour work week to run it efficiently.

Jim smiled coyly as Larry continued his repertoire on all of the reasons why his current job of overseeing operations would prevent him from heading up the Symphony project, but he listened intently, nodding and agreeing with everything Larry said. Then Larry took a deep breath and waited for Jim's response.

Jim sat on the corner of his desk, folded his arms and said, "I understand and I respect your commitment to your job, and the many hours you that you dedicate to it every week, Larry. That level of wholehearted devotion is exactly why I want you to head up Symphony. You are Mr. Implementation personified—you are the expert."

Larry began to launch another list of reasons why he could not head up the Symphony project, but Jim intervened.

"Larry, what was it you said in your presentation to us about the importance of putting the best possible people on the project? They are, and always will be, the very people you can least afford to have on the project. That fact especially applies to the person who can best lead this project"

Larry sat quietly for a moment before speaking.

"Jim, this is certainly a complement. Like everyone else on the team, I am concerned about the importance of having the right people in the right position. But, I am also worried about how my current department will run in my absence."

"I agree, Larry. That's exactly why your thoughts on making sure the project is properly planned out before it starts, including proper handovers to the people who will be filling in, are of critical importance. This may be more difficult than we initially thought, but this very conversation indicates that maintaining constant vigilance so we don't suddenly fall off the wagon is critical to its success. I think overcoming the hurdle of filling your shoes in operations in a highly efficient manner is a good example of a possible issue that can contribute to a failed project."

"I truly am honored Jim, and you're right—I need to think out of that 'obstacle' box. I agree, we can find the right person and give him or her the right training to handle my job the right way. And of course, I'll be on hand for any kind of support to keep things moving smoothly. I appreciate your confidence."

"Good," Jim reached out to shake Larry's hand. "Remember, Spencer is not performing well currently. We agree unanimously that putting the Symphony project into place will create significant improvement. I know you're the person to get this ball rolling and to prevent it from collecting any dust. You have my deepest confidence."

♪

As soon as the team reconvened following the break, Jim announced the appointment of Larry as head of Symphony at Spencer. He was straightforward and direct about why he had chosen Larry rather than others, such as Judi, who had already dedicated a lot of time and energy to the project and were highly qualified.

"It is imperative to have total openness and honesty among us throughout the entire project," Jim said to the team. "I do not want any water-cooler gossip or anyone feeling shunned. You all play a critical role in insuring that the Symphony project comes to full fruition. We will work as a chain; only as strong as its weakest link. But in the case of Symphony, you'll each have a welder in front and behind you for moments of weakness."

The discussion then lead to the difficulty Larry had seeing beyond his current role as head of operations. Jim pointed out that just this sort of "no-can-do" is a prime example of a weakened link. Everyone in the room agreed that it was easy to fall into this type of mindset.

"It's going to be a challenging journey," Judi offered. "Let's agree to call each other on any weakened link issues the very moment they occur. And, let's agree that we'll keep our egos and pride in check with the importance of Symphony's success. Let me be the first in the room to congratulate you, Larry. I'm proud to be your colleague."

Every other team member followed behind Judi with congratulatory words.

"Okay, good people," Jim said, calming the team back to silence. "We will meet again in about one week to discuss a detailed project plan that Larry will put together—with help from each of you—between now and then. His assistant will get the details of the meeting to you a couple of days in advance."

Chapter 8
The Project: Assessment and Implementation

Feeling slightly overwhelmed at the events that occurred during the previous hour, Larry sat at his desk absorbing all of the changes that were about to take place in his work life. Just that morning he was happily managing the company's operations department. Now he was responsible for heading up one of the most important projects the organization had ever engaged in.

He opened his notepad and started jotting notes to himself:

- Put the team together. Roles can change as we move forward, but it is important to structure the team based on having the right people involved who fit the Symphony criteria.

- Develop the Symphony infrastructure. Ensure there is enough time to do proper handovers with the people who will replace the team members in their current roles.

- Find someone to take control of operations while I am involved with the Symphony project. Speak with Jeremy Bridgehead.

Jeremy filled in for Larry during vacations and business trips. He knew the job, and he was the type of person who would grasp the opportunity with both hands. Larry noted to put together a handover document and plan so that Jeremy could get up and running quickly.

- Appoint the right people to analyze, design and implement the Symphony project. Meet with peers and colleagues to get suggestions of the best candidates.

- Develop the Symphony project context. Make sure that we as an executive team are able to constantly communicate about why we are going through this change and what it will men for the organization and the employees.

- Make sure all team members understand the events that lead to Spencer's current position so they will remain cognizant of and assist in preventing a recurrence or faltering in the Symphony reorganization project.

- Have Jim explain his Symphony epiphany to team members, and how the top management had committed to the project's development.

- Develop a plan to initiate and activate the project using the phase four approach developed by Judi; Current State Assessment, Future State Design, Implementation and Monitoring.

Larry further broke the phases down on paper. The objective of the first phase of assessment to be two-fold:

Establish to what extent Spencer was currently at as a Symphonic organization.

Assess the impact that initiating the Symphony project would have to the overall organization, i.e.; what is the expected uplift in company's performance if the issues uncovered in the assessment were successfully dealt with? Develop tools for accuracy in the assessment. The assessment will aid in determining how to best develop the design phase Following a normal design approach, it would include agreement of design specifications or criteria, high level design, detailed design, testing and modification

Determination of the most appropriate implementation would be impossible at the start of the project. It is important to determine if the entire organization should be engaged at one time, or if it should follow a phased approach with infield design in one of the departments first, followed by migration to other departments after proof of concept.

The team is ready!

Embed a solid change management and communication plan into the project, and continuously monitor results and speed and quality of implementation.

Draw a high level plan for Symphony.

The final note on Larry's pad read:

The Assessment

Larry sat at his desk compiling a list of deliverables for the assessment. We need to determine how well the organization is doing on all the key elements that make up a symphonic organization, he thought, as he started his list.

Symphony Element	Yes	No
Products and services are undisputedly superior		
Processes are clearly defined, updated and communicated. Employees follow the process precisely as it is written		
Each employee understands exactly how their performance affects the performance of others		
People must be supremely fit for their roles		
Significant amount of time and resources are devoted to training and re-training of employees		
The leaders of the organization must receive constant "real-time" information critiques on their performance		
Every performer is clear about the importance of their individual role to the complete project		
Promotions and advancements are based entirely upon performance		
Employees goals are team-based whenever possible		
Customers want one-stop shopping		
Expectations of employees are to be clear and comprehensible		
Performance against the expectations are to be measured continuously		
Customers want the best possible service and/or product, in the quickest possible time and at the lowest possible price		
Employees are hired and/or fired based on their required performance abilities to complete their tasks		
Managers and team leaders are not to engage in the manual work that the people on their teams are paid to do		

Symphony Element	Yes	No
Technology and systems must be in total support of the job performers as they carry out their roles		
Employees have an intimate understanding of the functioning of the tools they need to do their jobs, and technology and systems are continuously updated and refined to cater to customer's needs		
The team leader is imperative to the performance of the organization. His or her ability to lead and to anticipate and direct as performance occurs is critical to the performance of the organization		
The layout of the organization and the project progression should be closely linked to the design of the key processes		
Employees should know the minute they do a good or an unsatisfactory job		
The consequences of performance should be immediate, and tightly linked to the overall expectations of each employee		

Larry reasoned that, if after the assessment, team members and project participants answered in the affirmative to the questions posed in the list, it could be assumed that the organization process was as successful as possible, given the market circumstances at the given time.

If, however, the questions were not answered affirmatively, and Larry suspected that would likely be the case, the questions garnering negative answers would lead the organization towards a redesign that would improve performance significantly once implemented. The closure of the gaps identified in the assessment would drive the organization towards symphonic performance.

Note from the publisher: Look out for the fort-coming companion Symphony Tool-Kit book which will provide a comprehensive set of tools to implement Symphony in your organization or contact Stractics Group at www.stracticsgroup.com to attend one of their Symphony training programs or to speak with one of their advisors about how to implement Symphony in your organization.

♪

The assessment took just over five weeks. By the time it was completed, the picture had emerged clearly. Spencer's problems were a result of its organizational burdens, and it was in a precarious state. Larry had the task of reading the results to the entire management team:

Our products, with a few exceptions, are average for our industry, neither good nor bad. When compared with competitive solutions in the markets that we serve, our performance and products are merely average.

Our processes are simply broken. We do not document them. Everyone can, and in many cases they do follow their own—not the organization's—processes and procedures. And they do this with little or no consequences.

In many cases, our systems do not support our processes. In some cases, they actually hinder innovation.

Our managers spend far too much time doing their subordinates work. As a result, they do not spend enough time managing the performance of their subordinates.

Our managers and leaders do not have enough current and frequent information that enables them to properly lead their staff members. Information tends to be monthly, and it is frequently not accurate.

When it comes to functioning as a performance driven organization, there is a lot of room for improvement at Spencer. We talk frequently and in-depth about performance, but we continued, in some cases, to promote people based on longevity.

Larry continued through the laundry list of examples underpinning his findings. As he spoke, the mood in the room turned somber.

"I have asked repeatedly for new software to compile the stock reconciliations," said Judi.

Gary attempted to deflect Larry's comments about average products and services by launching an attack on the operations department.

"We can come up with the products, but you guys don't seem to be able to produce them for us Larry." Jim intervened, sensing that the meeting could turn controversial instead of productive.

"Okay guys, please stop and take a deep breath," he ordered. "This is not a question of who is at fault for the situation we find ourselves in. Let's just agree that it's entirely my fault and leave it at that. And I mean that honestly. It really is my fault. My role in this organization should be to simply enable you to do your jobs in the best possible way. It doesn't look like I've been able to do that, does it?

"But that's water under the bridge, and it's time to move forward in a positive and progressive way. The first thing we need to do is to come together as a team, and do what is best for the organization. Can we all come to a mutual agreement on this fact?"

Jim noted that every head in the room was nodding, accompanied by some low whispers of "yes." He continued, "As Larry and the team has just shown us, we have an opportunity which, conservatively speaking, could improve our profitability by about 20-percent. That's $30 million in one year! Is that something we're interested in accomplishing?"

With the situation quickly diffused, Jim knew the conversation could now turn to how to fix the issues reveled by Larry's analysis.

Six primary streams of work would be implemented. They agreed that there would be six major steams of work during the design phase:

• Product Development

• Process Improvement

• Systems and Technology

• Leadership Training

• Key Performance Indicators, Metrics and Performance Information Management

• Goal Translation/Expectation Settings

Each stream would be appointed its individual, dedicated team. Performance against milestones would be tightly measured during this phase. Because they felt that the Spencer organization was of a manageable size, the group chose to begin by planning for an implementation that would involve most of the departments in the company.

Jim's top team quickly realized they would need to change the existing analysis team. It would be necessary to augment it, or to move some members out to ensure that the right capabilities were brought to bear on the new design. Because of the systems' needs that had been identified, they decided to hire outside consulting expertise for some of the systems' development work required to be put into place.

♪

It took about seven weeks to complete the design phase. When it was completed, the work was ready to be tested in a live environment. During both the assessment and the design phases, the need to manage the change aspects of the project, including the communication aspects, became apparent. As the project progressed, it became obvious that these aspects were integral. During the process re-design work particularly, it was evident that people were beginning to worry about the security of their jobs. In some cases, this mindset resulted in incidents where team members attempted to circumvent the process of change.

Throughout the process, Jim, Larry and other top team members spent the majority of their time with groups of employees reassuring, cajoling and even, when necessary, pleading with them.

Sean McCoy, head of human resources, proposed the idea of playing classical music in the entrance foyer of all of the company's buildings so as people arrived at work every morning, they would be reminded that Spencer was in pursuit of symphonic performance. Classical music was soon playing in some of the work areas, as well as in the canteen. The music quickly became a primary driver of the change. But the music was not appealing to everyone, and some staff members complained. The music was confined to specific areas, such as hallways, lobbies and other common areas where people moved in and out of quickly. It continued to serve as a reminder of what the organization was in the process of implementing to everyone.

♪

At the end of the design phase, the team calculated the achieved changes.

The organization's key (mission critical processes):

The key processes had been redesigned and streamlined. In many cases, it had enabled the organization to offer guaranteed time-based performance. In almost every case, the company had outperformed other competitors in the marketplace. The processes were clearly documented and published to a central intranet site for easy updating and communication. The processes were now ready for use as a training tool. Once implemented, staff members would clearly understand what was expected of them, and of how their performance fit as a part of the overall picture.

Technology and enabling systems:

Driven by the redesign of the organization's mission critical processes, it became apparent during the design-phase that a new system was required to enable the processes to work as well as intended. In the current scenario, processes did not always communicate to each other clearly as they had been developed in a less than integrated fashion over time.

Products:

Marketing and sales representatives initiated a comprehensive customer and competitor study. As a result, several unmet needs were identified. Products were then designed to meet those needs. Sales staff who had seen the new products expressed excitement about the products' potential in the marketplace.

Leadership:

During the assessment, the issue of managers doing employee work was identified as a major impediment. During the design phase, a training program that all managers were required to take was developed to help them re-focus.

The top team felt that the leadership program would have a major impact on manager performance. In addition, a one-week course for Spencer's top 20 managers was designed with the help of the faculty of a leading university. The course was designed and developed to teach top-level managers the difference between leadership and management. The end result he intent was to develop leadership skills and convert the group into outstanding leaders.

Goal translation process:

As part of the design phase, a systematic performance objective process was designed for which all levels of the organization were required to sign off and agree to. Once implemented, the effect of the process would insure that everyone in the organization was clear and cognizant of the expectations the company placed upon them.

System for managing:

An issue of major importance was identified during the assessment; a lack of real-time information regarding performance.

In line with the new processes, capabilities of the new system, and the agreed process for translating goals and objectives, a system for managing performance was designed. This system included the metrics and key performance indicators that would be measured. In addition, management performance routines at each level of the organization would be reviewed, discussed and put into action.

Critical to the new management system, performance would be measured and managed as close as possible to the point in time in which the performance occurred. By upping the frequency of reviews, it was concluded that performance related issues could be avoided at the point of occurrence rather than after the incident.

♪

When the design phase was completed, the top team met again in an attempt to understand and agree to the team's proposals. During the meeting, the people on the various design teams presented and argued for their proposals for change. This had the corollary benefit of the design team members buying more deeply into the design in the process. The presentations sometimes resulted in heated debates among the top team members. But by the end of the meeting, everyone understood, and agreed to what was being designed.

Jim felt that prior to implementation was the time for him to meet with his boss, CEO, Eric Struber. It was, he felt, necessary to have Eric's buy-in to the new design before moving forward.

Just as he reached for the phone to call Pam, Eric's secretary, a thought struck him. Why not let my team present the design to Eric, rather than doing so myself? If Eric sees how strongly the team is dedicated to the design, he may be all the more convinced, and excited, to give his approval to move forward. At the same time, it would give the team a greater emotional connection to the project.

Jim dialed Pam's extension – 1

"Hi Pammy, it's your favorite son calling."

"Hi, favorite son. You can cut the compliments," she laughed. "I know you really just want to speak with the big man don't ya?" Your timing is good, he just walked in the office. Hold a sec, I'll connect you."

Eric greeted Jim warmly. "How is it going, Jim? You've been on my mind."

"I'm pleased with the progress, Eric," Jim responded and then offered a brief update on the program. "I feel it's time to show you what has been accomplished as of now. The team and I would like to make a presentation to you. I am hoping you can come to Spencer for a meeting soon."

"Sounds like you've made great progress, Jim. "I'll be happy to come, and to see first-hand where you are with the initiative," Eric offered. "This week's about over, and I have a pretty booked schedule for the rest of it. Let me pass you back to Pam and she'll etch it into my calendar for next week. Does that work for you?"

"Perfectly, Eric, thanks. We'll look forward to it."

The following week, the top team spent about four hours outlining the details of Spencer's new Symphony design for Eric. Each team-member presented his or her part of the design. Jim provided the overview of what the team had gone through from the initial epiphany of Symphony through the end of the design.

When the team finished, Eric asked several questions, and he offered a few suggested changes.

"It sounds like you guys are going to fundamentally change the way this organization works," Eric offered. "I think you've done a fantastic job so far. It this work is successful in the implementation phase, I will see to it that you get to feel the benefit during bonus time. But more importantly, I might have to call on some of you to help me implement Symphony in some of our other operating companies. It's up to you to bring this to a successful fruition now, and you have my full support. Make it work here, and you will have helped the entire organization. It's been an outstanding presentation, and I thank you."

Implementation

It was time to bring Symphony to a reality at Spencer. So far Jim and his team had determined what it would mean for the company to be managed in the same way a symphony is directed by its conductor. They had assessed the organization against the criteria, and had identified six major streams of work. And they had embarked on major redesign of the six areas. The necessary team was appointed, and the members and stakeholders had bought in to the new designs' implement. Now it was time.

Jim decided to make each of the top team members, including management systems and product development, responsible for one of the implementation streams, to ensure the continued buy-in and leadership of his one-downs. It was also to demonstrate to the rest of the organization that the top team continued to stand together in this quest to radically change the organization.

The implementation process that followed was a traditional project management process. First they would validate the design with key people at different levels of the organization. Next, a pilot or testing area where the design could be further refined was identified. Once the design had been fully tested, and any necessary modifications were made, the change would be cut over and fully implemented throughout the organization.

The team learned very quickly that, in many cases, it would be equally important to implement the new change and to stop the old way of doing things. If, for example, elements of an old process were still in place, it could be difficult at times for the people at the lowest level of the organization to let go of "the way we have always done it around here." Where the new design called for a radical change, and these issues became even more apparent, the team made sure to formally and systematically disengage the old way.

Not every step went smoothly during the implementation effort. Cynics, those who just wouldn't change, surfaced, but others were quick to embrace the changes. Some people were skeptical and asked a lot of questions. Through consistency and leadership the change was implemented.

During the process, Larry, who continued to manage the overall project, reflected. He had learned that the most important driver of a successful implementation was based on the determination and dedication of the team. No one was falling off the proverbial wagon. It was mutually important to every person to succeed, and they had learned that success depended on every one of them.

There were instances where people has to change their mindset or attitude to accommodate the change, but there were other instances where the people behind the change were being rewarded, and in some cases, promoted.

For Jim, this continued to be one of the most important and exciting times in his career. He had never before felt as energetic and in control of the outcome of the business performance.

♪

The team continued to measure the financial progress resulting from Symphony on a weekly basis through strict tracking of outcomes in the dedicated war-room. It wasn't long before they started seeing bottom line financial improvement beginning to materialize. Financial improvement was initially slow, but as change began to take hold on a broader scale throughout the organization, it became vigorous.

♪

Some people would say that implementation is never fully completed because there will always be the potential to tweak and further improve. At Spencer, the overall implementation took just under six months to complete. By then, new products had been launched, new processes were in place and new technology and systems were up and running. Where appropriate, old methods of doing business had been stopped. Leadership training had been conducted. Goals and objectives fully translated to all areas of the organization. A rigorous management information and performance management system was in place and working. Performance at the highest level of the organization continued on a weekly basis at a minimum, and in many cases they were conducted daily or even hourly at the frontline of the organization.

Conclusion

Six months after the initial implementation phase of Symphony, Jim and the team met to discuss the results with Eric. They placed a one-page brag-sheet in front of him:

- Revenues: up by 25-percent

- Overall market share: up by five-percent

- Overhead: up by five-percent

- Revenue/staff cost: up by 27-percent

- Number of customer complaints: down by 65-percent

- Average process turnaround time, re; improvement on five mission critical processes: 90-percent

- Labor turnover rate: During implementation, the initial turnover rate increased because of necessary staff changes. However, the turnover rate is now stabilized at a much lower level than normally experienced for the time of year.

- Health and safety incidents: down by 75-percent

♪

Eric sat at the conference table with the team in the same meeting room where they had met six months earlier. The room was silent when Jim placed the one-page list in front of Eric.

When Eric finally looked up, his eyes scanned those at the table, looking at each one in the eye. Then he turned to Jim. "All I can say is wow. Wow again," he grinned widely.

The team broke into a hearty laughter. "This is beyond my wildest expectations," Eric said. You guys have done it. Although I'm not exactly sure how, I owe you all a congratulations and a sincere thank you."

Jim stood and walked to the conference room door. He opened it and gestured to the pre-invited team-members who had been waiting outside to come into the meeting room. Almost 100 people crowded the room.

Jim waited for them to find a standing place, then motioned with his hands for quiet.

"My esteemed team, allow me to introduce you to Eric Struber, Spencer Holdings' CEO." He then turned to Eric.

"Eric, your congratulations and gratitude should be extended to everyone in this room. Without their commitment, championship, drive and determination, Symphony would not be the great success it is today."

Eric stood, and the silence deepened as everyone present focused their attention on him. He presented a short, but to the point speech. He thanked the team for their efforts and offered them congratulations. He concluded by announcing that a new role as regional CEO had recently been created in the holding company.

"Who do you think should get that job?" he asked.

"Jim! Jim! Jim!" the group's chants increased in volume with every call of Jim's name.

"It's my pleasure to announce that after a deserved vacation, Jim Robertson will be the new regional CEO of the central region which encompasses the three companies within the group that account for more than 65-percent of our profit."

The applause and whistles continued until Eric raised his hands motioning for calm. He then turned to Jim.

"You and your team have done an outstanding job, Jim," Eric continued. "I want you to implement Symphony in all the three companies. But, that means we will also need a new CEO at Spencer. It's my pleasure to announce Larry Cummings as Spencer's new chief executive officer."

Jim and Larry stared at each other wide-eyed, with broad grins across their faces.

"And finally," Eric continued, "it is my great pleasure to, for the second time, to present Jim Robertson with the Most Valuable Player award. This is the first time in our history that a person has been award with this honor twice. Congratulations Jim, Well done."

Post Script

Ahh, Jim contemplated two weeks later. Bora Bora. The blue lagoon. Snorkeling. Romantic walks on the beach with Jill. Orions Belt. The Southern Cross. The music of Tchaikovsky. Ahh, life is good.

Post Script